I Did It
His Way

to Alex

May you know the love
of God in your life

Romans 8:39

Hugh Ident

Front cover

My grateful thanks to David Ash of CPO for designing the front cover: perhaps a few words of explanation would be helpful. It is a montage representing the murkiness of my past life and the turmoil and confusion I went through on my journey to a life of trust, honour and love as I came to know the reality of Jesus Christ. The drink is self-evident; the pound notes, large Roland Ultra printing press and tins of ink represent the commercial world I was part of for many years; the Bible represents the spiritual world I discovered and my call into the ministry. The house is the family home in Glasgow; Glasgow and Worthing are the locations where much of the story took place.

Hugh Hill

I Did It *His* Way

Hugh Hill

H & J Publishing

Published by H & J Publishing
8 Albion Crescent
Lincoln LN1 1EB

Website: www.hjpublishing.co.uk
Email: hugh@hjpublishing.co.uk

Unless otherwise stated Scripture quotations are taken from The Holy
Bible, New International Version. Copyright © 1973, 1978, 1984 by
International Bible Society. Used by permission of Hodder and
Stoughton Limited.

KJV – King James Version. Crown copyright.

ISBN 978-0-9562187-0-4

Typeset by CRB Associates, Reepham, Norfolk
Cover design by David Ash, CPO, with some creative input from Vicki Hill
Printed and bound by CPI Antony Rowe, Chippenham and Eastbourne

CONTENTS

Due to the remarkable series of events
that led me into the Christian life, the subsequent
wonderful answers to prayer and the way they
radically affected my business and home life,
I was advised to record a cassette diary.
This I did and what follows is transcribed
from these tapes.

Acknowledgments

This is the story of a sequence of events covering twenty-nine years. The story begins in Glasgow then moves to Worthing, London and finally to Lincoln. It obviously involves many people to whom I owe an immense debt of gratitude. Some are mentioned in this book and others, whose names do not appear in print, will recognise the part they played in my story. There are many, many others, whose lives briefly touched and influenced mine; you, too, are remembered with thanks.

The 'hero' of this book is unquestionably our great and mighty Father God. My 'Damascus Road' encounter with Him on Friday evening 30th April, 1982, has never been forgotten nor has its impact lessened with the passing of the years. Yes, as I say in the book, with the benefit of Bible training and pastoral experience I would probably do many things differently, but I would always want to do them *His* way.

Hugh Hill

CHAPTER 1

SETTING THE SCENE

I stood poised one step away from the edge of the abyss, about to step forward into the void and lose everything near and dear to me, and the hellish thing was I couldn't see it!

Frozen with fear, I stood transfixed by the vision before me and knew with an awful certainty that was where my life was heading ...

A forty-two-year old man, having the outward appearances of achievement: a large comfortable home and my own business with all the material benefits that brings. Yet for all this confident assurance, I was lost in my own materialistically driven world, and blind to all the problems caused by my alcohol-fuelled life-style. I stood poised one step away from the edge of the abyss, about to step forward into the void and lose everything near and dear to me, and the hellish thing was I couldn't see it!

Let me take you back in time and tell you the circumstances leading up to this miraculous life-changing experience. I was forty-two years of age, married with three children and managing director of my own printing company. A member of the Institute of Marketing with a background of sales in the printing/packaging industry I had worked extensively throughout the United kingdom. Career minded, hard working and ambitious, I had learned how hard work did lead to advancement if you applied yourself to the task at hand.

You often hear it said that, 'If you remember the sixties you weren't there.' That's just clever talk. In truth, outside the 'beatnik, hippy' life-style of a minority, the majority were enjoying the new-found freedom of cultural revolution in the swinging sixties. The newly available wealth brought almost unlimited job prospects and opportunities for those who were ambitious and eager, in the phrase of the day, 'to get on' in booming Britain. Glasgow was no exception. Yes, traditional industries were facing severe competition and would close, but to borrow a phrase from Prime Minister Harold Wilson, the 'white hot heat of new technology' was opening new and exciting opportunities. Bob Dylan told us 'the times were a-changin'' and the Beatles sang 'all you need is love'. So, for the generation in its early twenties who had come through the dull and depressing post-war years, the sixties were an exciting and liberating time in which to live.

Like many of my generation I had attended Sunday school in the 1940s and enjoyed the companionship of the Boys' Brigade in the 1950s, but I had never experienced what born-again Christians call a 'personal relationship with Jesus'. To me religion was a 'crutch for those who needed it'. I certainly did not, and by the 1960s I was aiming for all the things the world counts as important and had no time for church. With leisure activities such as sailing and golf, and sufficient disposable income, life was to be enjoyed. The companionship of like-minded friends encouraged me in the play-hard, work-hard philosophy of life, and business entertaining encouraged drinking to excess.

In retrospect, I now see how I failed to realize that in my early twenties I had all the obvious symptoms of a potential problem drinker: binge drinking, alcohol always present and a tendency to gravitate towards friends with similar views on alcohol consumption.

As the years passed, the combination of the Scottish drink culture, business entertaining, the pressure of leading my company through the vicious manufacturing recession of the eighties and a busy social and family life, meant my personal consumption of alcohol grew to alarming proportions. And while in my heart of hearts I knew I was drinking too much, I really couldn't get off the carousel. On the occasions when well-meaning friends would warn me about the damage I was causing to my marriage, family, health and business, I would tell them, 'It was none of their business, it was my life and I would live it as I chose, I worked hard and I would play hard!'

I often look back and reflect with amazement at the stubborn blindness of men and women who, like me, sense their lives are sliding out of control but are unable to admit their weaknesses or accept their need of help. I guess it's all the more difficult when you have some of the trappings of success and appear to have achieved much of what society admires and aims for. Later I would understand the deception of living to the world's agenda and what the apostle Paul called the 'veil over our minds' that prevents us from seeing the truth (see 2 Corinthians 4:3–4).

Joyce . . .

*I put on a brave face outside the home
but the pressure increased to the point where
I realized our marriage was heading for breakdown.*

My husband worked long hours and did a lot of business entertaining that gave him an excuse to drink heavily, which led to problems with our marriage and family life. I put on a brave face outside the home but the pressure increased to the point where I realized our marriage was heading for breakdown. I even visited the doctor who understood what I was going through but could only offer me pills to keep me calm, but I preferred to try to cope on my own. Eventually the tension and strain became too much, and one Friday evening, 30th April, when my husband came home late and 'high' as usual, I left him at home in charge of the children, something I had never done before, and went to visit my mother. The minister of the local parish church, Rev. Lawless, was paying a call, and when he asked how I was, I burst into tears and told him about the situation. He told me of a couple he knew who had been in similar circumstances and how God had intervened and totally turned their situation around. Although I heard what he said I didn't feel this had anything to do with me. He then prayed for Hugh and me, and as he was praying I also prayed, silently pleading, 'God if You are there, please give me the strength I need to cope with what lies ahead.' I felt sure my marriage was about to break and I didn't know how to cope. This all took place around 8.00 pm.

CHAPTER 2

THE SUPERNATURAL EXPERIENCE

The temperature was extraordinarily cold and
I stood transfixed by the vision surrounding me.
I was freezing cold, scared witless and
utterly overcome with dread.

It was Friday evening, 30th April. Having had a drink after work as usual, which led to an argument with my wife, Joyce had gone to visit her mother who lived in the west-end of Glasgow. My oldest daughter was at the Girl Guides, my son was at the Cubs and my youngest daughter asleep in bed.

Around 8.00 pm I had a terrifying experience: I had a vision of what, at the time, I imagined to be hell. I have only ever been able to describe it as resembling the moonscape when we viewed it on black and white television during the lunar landings of the 60s and 70s. It was a cold landscape, dark and horrible, but somehow alive and very frightening. The temperature was extraordinarily cold and I stood transfixed by the vision surrounding me. I was freezing cold, scared witless and utterly overcome with dread.

When discussing religion I had often asked the question, 'Why, if there was a God, did He waste time with Church and Jesus and all the rest of it, and not just do something impressive to prove the Christian message was true?' Right then I knew with a dreadful certainty that God was in fact 'doing something'. He was showing me where my life was heading. Then, surprisingly, for it's not something I would ever normally have thought of doing, I had an overwhelming desire to read the Bible. My mother had given me a Bible when I was twenty-one years of age and I hadn't opened it in all these years. If asked, I would have said, 'I don't have a Bible.' Yet, following an impulse, I walked to a bookcase slid open the glass door and put my hand behind the books to grasp that very Bible given to me all those years ago. I took it out and it fell open at the Gospel of John. My eyes went to the verse in John 1:5 that spoke of the 'light' (meaning Jesus), who had come into the world to shine through the spiritual darkness. I cannot begin to explain it, but the Bible in my hand was like a lifebelt and even with the frightening vision still around me somehow I felt safe.

I then had what I can only call 'an inner prompting' to phone a neighbour who I knew was a Christian. Over the years he had pestered me to go to evangelistic events at his church. Having refused him numerous times I would then feel guilty, and not wanting to hurt him I would go along to some church event to please him but I was always glad when it was over. I spoke to him on the telephone and asked him to come to my house as soon as possible. He arrived within minutes, to be met by me standing on the doorstep trembling and frightened. Together we went inside where, to my surprise, he could see nothing of the vision which still surrounded me. I told him what had happened and he spoke about God and the Bible, and prayed. As his words flowed, the vision disappeared, the temperature rose too, and, although shaken, I felt much calmer. After a while, not quite certain what was happening, he left and soon afterwards my wife, Joyce, returned home.

I began to tell her what had happened, and understandably she put it down to my drinking (wouldn't you?). So, confused and provoked with that all-too-familiar self-pitying feeling when you think that if you're being blamed for doing something you didn't do, you may as well do it anyway, I made my way to a local hotel to have a drink.

But it was not to be. When I reached the street corner a voice quite unmistakably within me, in a sort of bemused 'father to wayward child' tone, asked, 'Where are you going?' and nudged me back in the direction of home. Now I had never experienced anything remotely like this before and strangely, rather than fear, I felt a sense of peace. Something extraordinary was happening to me and I knew everything was going to be all right.

Back home, I sat down with Joyce and she told me that while visiting her mother that evening, the local Church of Scotland minister had paid a visit. When he asked how life was with her, she had broken down in tears as she described the situation at home: my drinking and the damage it was doing to our marriage and family. The minister said, 'Joyce, all I can offer you is prayer.' Joyce then told me that he prayed for her, for me and for the family.

Astonished, and sensing that this was directly related to my own experience earlier that evening, I asked Joyce, 'What time did this happen?' She replied, 'About 8 o'clock.' I then excitedly exclaimed, 'Well, you should hear what happened here about 8 o'clock,' and related the evening's events to my wife.

Now Joyce and I were not Christians: we weren't even religious and we didn't attend church. In fact, I was suspicious and mistrusted anything to do with church-goers and would argue enthusiastically against the Christian religion. Yet, in a complete about turn, my extraordinary vision, linked with Joyce's coincidentally answered prayer, seemed to break through the fog of cluttered thinking and confirmed what I had secretly suspected over the years but never allowed myself to think nor dare to voice: that perhaps the Christian religion was true after all.

Since then I have often witnessed the miraculous way in which men and women suddenly and unexpectedly change their thinking from long-held convictions against Christianity to complete acceptance. Even though there is much they don't understand and though they still have many questions unanswered, they know with an inner certainty that the Christian message is true. The questions that were once a barrier to faith and seemed to be so important, now in the light of their newly found conviction do not seem important after all.

Later, I was to learn how the apostle Paul, in Romans 1, speaks of God's invisible qualities, saying that all men and women know the truth about God yet choose to suppress it. In other words, deep down we know God is real, and no matter how much we argue against Jesus and say we don't believe in God, we know He is who He says He is. When we look at the stars, at a new-born baby or a flower, we know there is a Creator God. For as the writer to the Ecclesiastes says:

'He has made everything beautiful in its time. He has also **set eternity in the hearts of men**; yet they cannot fathom what God has done from beginning to end.'

(Ecclesiastes 3:11, emphasis added)

It's that God-shaped spiritual emptiness in our hearts that longs to be filled. This explains why men and women who profess not to believe in God and Christianity will pray to Jesus in times of great trial. Although they normally scoff at the devil, angels, miracles and Jesus, they will happily embrace the concept of UFOs, spiritism, astrology, magic, witchcraft and New Age practices. Literally, belief in anything rather than Christ.

Somehow all of that truth produced a song in my heart, and Joyce and I sat and talked into the night. We didn't know exactly what was happening to us but felt we were going through some sort of spiritual awakening. As we talked we recalled, as if from a past and distant life, how we had both responded to Billy Graham's invitation to accept Jesus in 1956 at Glasgow. I had gone forward at the Ibrox Football Stadium and Joyce had done so at the Kelvin Hall. We both clearly remembered a genuine personal response to an inner summons. In another strange 'co-incidence' it transpired that both Joyce and I were baptised into the Church of Scotland in 1959. Yet we had both fallen away and by the time we met in the early sixties neither of us was remotely religious.

So, late that Friday night as I prepared for bed, my mind was a mixture of fear, apprehension and confusion. As I walked into my bedroom, to my consternation and delight, I saw a pocket New Testament lying on my pillow. My fourteen-year-old daughter had come home from the Guides and, having overheard something of the conversation, looked in the lounge and saw the open Bible on the coffee table. Knowing I didn't have an up-to-date version, Jacqui found a modern pocket New Testament and left it on my pillow. Jacqui had accepted Jesus as her Saviour when she was eight years old but I had seen this as a 'childish phase' and so did nothing to encourage her in her faith. But she believed, attended Sunday school, and prayed for her Mum and Dad. I cannot adequately express how I felt that night when I went to sleep holding that New Testament in my hand. I didn't fully grasp all that was taking place but I knew that the Bible and what it represented for me was 'safe'. I slept soundly, unaware of the far-reaching changes about to take place in my life and the lives of my family.

The next day I awoke and discovered to my amazement that my desire for alcohol had gone. At that stage I was drinking not far short of a bottle of whisky a day. I went to the kitchen cupboard brought out the bottle and poured it down the sink, telling Joyce, 'I don't know what's happening to us but I know this no longer plays any part in our lives.'

I've often looked back to that moment and realized that God is a God of miracles for those who have eyes to see and ears to hear, and not believing means not seeing. This truth should be a wonderful encouragement for those who pray for God to intervene in the lives of their loved ones, and it should give hope to those who want God to break in and release them from habits and addictions which degrade their lives.

On Saturday afternoon something really extraordinary occurred and it was only years later when I was at Bible college that I was able to appreciate the theological significance of what happened that weekend.

I visited the local newsagent's shop, and lying on the counter was a pornographic book which I recognised as one that my friends had said I should read. There it was in front of me. It's important to understand that this local newsagent would never have that type of book for sale, and most definitely not lying openly on the counter. I can't explain this but I do not believe that book was there for anyone else to see. A voice within me told me to go ahead and buy the book. Now remember, I had no Christian friends as such, no Bible knowledge or church background to help me understand what was taking place, and given the life-style I was used to it would have been quite the norm for me to purchase the book. However, another inner voice cautioned, 'No!' It wasn't that I heard a voice saying, 'This is Jesus calling.' What I can say is the voice was 'clean'. I know, I know, how can a voice be 'clean'? Later I was to learn that it was because it was the Holy Spirit speaking to my spirit and I acknowledged purity and holiness as being 'clean'. What I did know, without any shadow of doubt, was that if I bought the book then all that had happened over the previous twenty-four hours would be put down to high blood pressure or something like that, my life would continue as before, and the previous night's vision would count for nothing. I also sensed that if, on the other hand, I did not buy the book, my life would radically change. At that time I had no sense of following Jesus or even becoming a Christian. I knew nothing about being 'born again'. All I knew was that I wanted to obey the 'clean' voice and thus didn't buy the book.

When I woke the following Sunday morning I had an overwhelming desire to attend church. Never having visited any local churches I knew nothing about them. However, there was a Church of Scotland church in our neighbourhood and I decided to go there.

I was somewhat nervous about walking into a church by myself and suggested to my ten-year-old son that perhaps he would come to church with me. Isn't that amazing? Here was a self-assured, forty-two-year-old man of the world, who called Christianity a 'crutch' and derided churchgoers, anxious about going to church. Much later I realized just how much of a spiritual battle this is.

Walking through the doorway of the church building a voice spoke clearly within me and quietly whispered, 'Welcome home.' Into my mind came the memory of my response to Billy Graham and the realization that, though I had forgotten about God, God had never forgotten about me, and I sensed Him say, 'Welcome home.' I listened to the minister's sermon and though it didn't mean much to me at the time, what did make an impact was him reading from the Bible a portion of Romans chapter 8. When he came to the passage beginning at verse 35 and reaching its climax in verse 39 with the glorious truth that *'neither height nor depth, nor anything else in all creation, will be able to separate us from the love of God that is in Christ Jesus our Lord'*, I began silently to weep.

Now the Bible tells us in Romans 10:17 that *'faith comes from hearing the message, and the message is heard through the word of Christ'*. Up until that point in all that had been happening to me since Friday night I had not allowed the Word of God to speak to me. But now, sitting in tears in that church pew, thinking of what I had heard whispered into my heart as I entered the church, and what God had said to me from Romans chapter 8, I was convicted of my sin and convinced of my need of Jesus to save me from the hellish future awaiting me in my vision on Friday night.

Suddenly I 'saw it'. Where before there had been spiritual darkness and inconclusive discussions about Christianity that always ended with pointless questions about dinosaurs, other faiths, or why God allowed suffering – all awkward pegs upon which to hitch anti-Christian views – I now realized that God loved me, and loved me so much He sent His Son to die for me. And most importantly, as Jesus had died for my sins by paying the price I deserved to pay, I was forgiven and my debt was paid. I was saved! Some lines from Charles Wesley's classic hymn 'And can it be...' summed up my intense emotion:

I woke, the dungeon flamed with light.
My chains fell off, my heart was free;
I rose, went forth, and followed Thee.

After the church service, following my wife's advice, I went to see the Christian who had visited me on Friday night. I explained to him all that had happened on Saturday and at church on Sunday. He then understood that God was taking me through the conversion experience and calling me into His kingdom. He told me of Saul's dramatic conversion experience on the road to Damascus recorded in Acts chapter 9 and how he became the apostle Paul. I listened to the explanation and understood what I had to do. I confessed my sin to God, asked for His forgiveness and for Jesus to be my Saviour and Lord. I was later to learn that this was the 'born-again' experience by which, following repentance for sin and acceptance of Jesus as personal Saviour, the Holy Spirit indwells the human 'heart' and reconciles us to God. So, at forty-two years of age I became a Christian. Upon returning home I told Joyce what I had done, and praise God, she did the same. Together we entered a new life, little knowing all the exciting changes God had in store for us.

A Daughter's Testimony
Dr Jacqueline C. Hill MBChB, MRCOG, PhD

I was coming home in the evening as late as possible, as was my habit, and while walking up the driveway to the house I 'felt', really felt, that something was different, something had changed. I let myself in and went up the stairs to the living room where my Dad would usually be with his whisky. My Dad wasn't there and beside my Dad's chair, instead of the usual bottle was an open Bible. Then I knew with 100% certainty that God had visited my Dad.

I cannot remember a time in my life when I was not conscious of God. I had a best friend when I was eight years old and her family were Christians and went regularly to church. She and her brothers went to Sunday school and sometimes my brother and I went with them. At other times my aunt took us, but apart from Christmas nativity plays and Easter services, my parents did not go to church.

At Sunday school I became aware that Jesus Christ, God's Son, had died on the cross for me, to take the punishment that I deserved and to enable me to live in relationship with Him. Certainly, aged eight, I didn't understand it all (aged thirty-eight, I still don't understand it all!) but I understood enough to find myself one night praying in bed, asking God to forgive me for the things I had done wrong and asking Jesus to come and live in me. From that time forward I discovered I could talk to God and know His presence in my life as my friend as well as my Father and my God and I determined to live my life for Him.

As a child, I remember conversations with my father who told me some of his sci-fi theories about God; for example, perhaps God was actually a computer in the sky launched millions of years ago when the world was more advanced than it is now, but then war had wiped out the human race and the knowledge of the computer had been lost! From these conversations I deduced that my father did not have the relationship with God that I had and I started to pray for him and for my Mum.

In my early teenage years, my Dad, who always drank heavily (as had his father before him), really started to show signs of addiction. He was often drunk when he arrived home, his behaviour was very unpredictable and sometimes frightening, and the relationship between him and my Mum started to deteriorate. I can remember trying to stay out of the house for as long as possible and stay out of the way as much as I could. I began to dread the shouting and started to hate my parents; my Dad for his drinking and my Mum for her anger towards him. I tried to pray harder. I prayed every day and I read my Bible every day but the situation at home only became worse. Eventually, I started to be angry with God too

and accused Him of not caring about us, of not
loving us. I gave God an ultimatum: 'If You don't
want to help us then I don't want to talk to You any
more.' I put my Bible away on the top shelf and I
stopped praying.

Then followed probably one of the most miserable
years of my life. I was fourteen. I remember clearly
the night God reached out to my Dad:

I was coming home in the evening as late as
possible, as was my habit, and while walking up the
driveway to the house I 'felt', really felt, that
something was different, something had changed.
I let myself in and went up the stairs to the living
room where my Dad would usually be with his
whisky. My Dad wasn't there and beside my Dad's
chair, instead of the usual bottle was an open Bible.
Then I knew with 100% certainty that God had
visited my Dad. God had answered my prayers and I
had been the one to give up, not Him. For an instant
I felt awful. I had doubted God, I had given up . . .
but that fleeting feeling of sorrow was swept away in
an incredible feeling of joy and awe. (I've often
thought that maybe this will be the way it is when
we get to heaven – the fleeting sorrow of all that we
gave up on, all the times we doubted Him and didn't
trust Him, and then all these things just swept away
in the incredible joy of His presence.)

Anyway, where was my Dad? I heard voices in the
lounge, the door was closed and I didn't want to
intrude so I just peeked through the edge and saw
Mum and Dad talking about Jesus and Christianity.
What could I do to help encourage him? The open
Bible I had seen was an old English version which I

thought would be difficult for him to understand, so off I went to my bedroom to find my Gideon's Bible, written in modern English and with an index at the back showing where to find help when . . . I put this on his bedside table and went off to my bed, taking my Bible back down from the shelf and thanking God for what he had done.

That was a Friday night. I can't remember anything about the following Saturday but I do remember on Sunday that in the afternoon Dad took my brother and me to the home of my best friend and left us to play with the other children while he talked with my friend's father.

Then started a new life for all of us. An upside-down family turned the right way up!

A Neighbour Remembers
Ian L. Macdonald BDS

. . . realizing something very unusual was happening; hurrying round to Hugh's house to find him waiting on his doorstep, clutching a Bible, afraid to go back into the house and literally shaking with fear; clasping my hand for what seemed an age as with great emotion and agitation he described the supernatural event he had experienced. The dominant impression, however, was that a real sense of the fear of God had come upon Hugh.

The Hill family moved into our neighbourhood on the south side of Glasgow in 1971. We soon got to know them, as their children were friendly with our

children and in the same class in first the local
primary and then later the local secondary school.
We also met weekly at a family swimming club for
residents in the area.

Because of her friendship with our daughter,
Jacqui Hill started attending our church Sunday
school in Pollokshaws and at the age of eight trusted
Jesus as her Saviour and King. This significant event
encouraged my wife and me to pray regularly for her
parents. Joyce showed some interest in the gospel
but Hugh was different: he was very much the
self-made man, assured and a little cynical about
anything religious. Christianity was not for the
managing director of a printing firm! He did,
however, respond, perhaps a little reluctantly, to a
few invitations to attend Christian events: a Sunday
school prize-giving, an evangelistic 'Friends &
Neighbours' evening, a debate between a Christian
in education and the socialist shop steward Jimmy
Reid (of Upper Clyde Shipbuilders fame), and the
testimony of one of the first astronauts to stand on
the moon come to mind. These irregular occasions
seemed to be the sum total of anything Christian in
Hugh's life, at least until the evening of Friday,
30th April, 1982.

That dramatic night remains vividly etched in my
mind: the urgent phone call from Hugh to 'Come
quickly'; kneeling for a brief prayer with my wife,
realizing something very unusual was happening;
hurrying round to Hugh's house to find him waiting
on his doorstep, clutching a Bible, afraid to go back
into the house and literally shaking with fear;
clasping my hand for what seemed an age as with

great emotion and agitation he described the
supernatural event he had experienced. The
dominant impression, however, was that a real sense
of the fear of God had come upon Hugh.

Eventually, things calmed down enough for us to
go inside, where Hugh shared some of the problems
he faced in his marriage, at work and with drink.
(Joyce had walked out that evening after yet another
row to go to her mother's on the west side of the
city.) But in the great darkness that had engulfed him
that evening, he had found a Bible and phoned a
Christian friend. For the next hour or so I shared
from that Bible the good news of the gospel of Jesus
Christ before leaving after prayer. As promised, I
phoned the following day anxious to discover how
he saw the events of the previous evening. I found
that not only was God working in Hugh's life but
also in that of his wife, Joyce. Her visit to her mother
had coincided with a visit from her Church of
Scotland minister. He had been praying with her,
after she had unburdened her deep concerns to him,
at the very same time as, across the city, I had been
praying with Hugh! Such is the amazing sovereign
providence of our God.

I met with Hugh the following day and
explained God's plan of salvation, and there in the
front room of our house Hugh prayed, willingly
committing his life to Jesus Christ as his Saviour and
Lord. In that moment he had passed from death to
life, come out of the darkness into the light. Joyce
needed little encouragement to do the same, and
when her husband returned home to tell her of
what he had done, she readily made her own

decision to respond to the grace of God revealed in the gospel.

So a new life had begun which was soon to manifest itself in a number of different ways. For example, church, which was once seen as an irrelevant crutch for those who needed it, now became their joy and delight! The never-opened Bible was eagerly and read daily, prayer became a must, Hugh's drink problem was solved overnight by being given strength to go teetotal, the children had reconciled parents with a new found love for each other, Hugh had a great desire to share his new faith with his colleagues and employees and to use his printing firm to help further the spread of the gospel, and pride and self-confidence were replaced with a humble trust and dependency on God!

Weekly, for a period of almost two years, my wife Jean and I met with Hugh and Joyce to help them grow in their relationship with Jesus Christ and build a firm Christian foundation for future service. We prayed together over the difficulties they faced and the opportunities God gave them, and sought to direct their great enthusiasm according to the priorities of the Bible. A few months after their Christian conversion we witnessed their baptism, along with that of their daughter Jacqui (then fourteen) in Greenview Evangelical Church, Glasgow. It was a great day. I vividly recall the tears of joy as they stood together, dripping wet watching Jacqui's baptism and singing the hymn, 'How great Thou art'.

Looking back, our hearts are filled with thankfulness to God for His amazing grace and we rejoice in the humble privilege of being workers

together with Him. Eternity will reveal the full
extent of how He uses human lives in achieving His
saving purposes, but the rest of this book will open
your eyes to the possibilities as you see how He uses
ordinary people (and late starters!) like Hugh and
Joyce for His greater glory.

Joyce...

*A new life began for our family, and step-by-step a total
transformation took place with Christ in control. My
prayer for strength was answered that Friday evening.
As the Bible says, God 'is able to do immeasurably more
than all we ask or imagine' (Ephesians 3:20).*

Scripture has a wonderful promise from God: *'Before
they call I will answer'* (Isaiah 65:24). I was to discover
the truth of that for myself that evening.

When I returned home Hugh seemed somewhat
disturbed. He said that he had had a strange
experience and was going for a walk to clear his head.
I called my sister-in-law (she is now a believer) and
while we were talking Hugh returned home. We sat
down and he recounted the events of his evening. He
told me an amazing story of what he had experienced
around the same time that Rev. Lawless had been
praying for us. We didn't understand what was
happening but we were aware that it was something
spiritual. Eventually, we went to bed to discover a
Bible lying on Hugh's pillow. (Our then fourteen-
year-old daughter, Jacqui, a believer, had overheard
some of our conversation and put the Bible there.)

The outcome of that incredible evening was a gradual understanding of God's power in our lives. A Christian friend and neighbour who had been praying for us, was instrumental in showing us, through the Bible, our need of Jesus. This led to our repentance and a wonderful awareness of sins forgiven. A new life began for our family, and step-by-step a total transformation took place with Christ in control. My prayer for strength was answered that Friday evening. As the Bible says, God *'is able to do immeasurably more than all we ask or imagine'* (Ephesians 3:20).

My husband's desire for alcohol left him to be replaced by a desire for the true Spirit: the Spirit of God Himself. We joined a local church fellowship where we studied the Bible and were encouraged to seek God and share what we discovered of Him. We attended every meeting we could, from all-age Bible school to Saturday morning prayer meetings. Our children were blessed and each, in time, professed belief in Jesus. Hugh and I, together with our oldest daughter, were baptised on 29th August. What a wonderful day that was.

The printing company grew and we saw God working wonderfully among the folks we worked with, as well as in our wider family. We had so many wonderful blessings. Day by day we watched His hand guide us. We had many struggles and went through many puzzling times as He taught us to trust Him more and I learned the truth of the saying that, 'With God there are many mysteries but no mistakes.'

CHAPTER 3

THE DAWN OF A NEW DAY

*A radical conversion experience generally produces
a mixed reaction from friends and family.
In my own case, some were sympathetic,
some resentful, some confused, and some even
offended, but a few recognised that something
'not of this world' had happened and
there was no earthly use in fighting it.*

With alcohol removed from my life God brought a new-found love and happiness into our marriage and family: a miraculous transformation. I now understood my eldest daughter's love for Jesus, and Joyce, Jacqui and I were baptised in August of that same year (1982). But I run ahead of myself.

The Monday following the weekend of my conversion and acceptance of Jesus Christ as my Saviour and Lord, I went to work as usual. Only this time something important had to be attended to first.

My works manager was a deacon in the Baptist Church, and was the only person in my workplace who professed to have a personal faith in Jesus. When I arrived at the factory I went directly to him and explained what had happened over the weekend and how I had become a Christian. With tears in his eyes he wrapped his arms around me and said, 'Thank God!' There we were in the middle of the factory floor, the works manager crying tears of joy, hugging the managing director! He told me, 'Now I know why God has kept me in this godless place for so long. I've asked Him so often to move me from here. Now I know why He didn't.'

This Christian colleague was to be a great source of help and advice for me in the early stages of my new life, particularly when I needed answers to the many questions that arose in my everyday life as a new Christian. Something I was to discover in the years ahead is that God's timing is perfect and He has His people in the places where He wants them to be of use for Him to fulfil His particular plans and purposes. This, of course, is of immeasurable help to the young in faith who need wisdom and guidance as they move out into the new Christian life. Conversely, it is also a great blessing to mature Christians as it increases their assurance and understanding of God's ways, thus giving them the pleasure of knowing they are being used to build His kingdom.

The fact that becoming a Christian means entering a radical, new and different life-style became very apparent when the Sunday following our conversion experience Joyce and I and our three children went along to Greenview Evangelical Church, where the Christian neighbour who had been so helpful the previous weekend was an elder.

It's hard to explain to the lifelong churchgoer just how alien a church service can be to new believers. We were completely out of our comfort zone, our hearts were hammering and we were aware of being strangers in uncharted waters. We listened to unfamiliar hymns and songs, and began to learn new words and concepts. Yet the warmth and friendliness of other Christians, their obvious understanding of our feelings, and their open and honest confession of how they too had once been where we were now calmed many a fear and allowed us to focus our attention on the Christian faith: growing in love and knowledge of Jesus and bringing our lives under His control.

Past attendance at church services had always been as a reluctant guest at Christmas or on other special occasions. During these services I had been aware of 'them' getting at me so my guard had been up allowing every childhood and boyhood prejudice to hold sway. I can't help thinking now how silly it was. I mean, when people make the fact that they were 'made to go to Sunday school', or 'went to church three times on Sunday' their excuse for not going to church, all they are doing is allowing mixed-up badly-informed childhood emotions to influence their adult decisions, which, when you think about it, can have eternal consequences. That was how I responded; I mentally switched off and looked forward to escaping from 'church' back into the 'real world'. But not now. Not now I was born again. Now the deepest longing of my soul was to know God and to worship Him and the obvious place to do that was in the company of fellow believers in a local Bible-believing church. The same is true for all Christians.

I was still a heavy cigarette smoker. I knew intellectually that I should stop for my health's sake and I disliked the thought of being dependent on anything other than Jesus. But having failed to stop smoking many times in the past I was reluctant to make another attempt. A wise Christian said to me, 'After all the changes God has made in your life, just be patient. When God is ready He will tell you when to stop!' So, for a number of months a bone-china saucer was provided as an ashtray as I continued my habit in homes where the smell of tobacco smoke was unknown. And, yes, one day I sensed it was time to stop.

We were planning a summer holiday at the Keswick Christian Convention in the company of other church families. I knew I would be expected to climb the surrounding Lakeland hills and would not be able to do so unless I stopped smoking. So, bearing in mind my many, many failed attempts to kick the habit, I spoke directly to God. 'Lord,' I said, 'I sense You want me to stop smoking, and I want to. I know I lack the strength to make it happen, but You don't. You have already proved this by removing my addiction to alcohol and radically changing my life-style. So here's what I'll do, Lord. Tomorrow morning I will not buy cigarettes as I usually do, and providing I have no craving I will never buy cigarettes again. But if I have that awful nerve-end craving I will not fight it, for I know I will be unable to resist buying cigarettes.' I added, 'Lord, I am not being presumptuous, but if I have to fight the craving in my own strength, it's foolish, for I know You have the power to do it for me!' The following morning when I went to work I did not stop to buy cigarettes, and have never experienced a craving for tobacco since.

The change in my life-style obviously affected some of my old friendships. Remember, I was forty-two and had lots of friends with whom I had enjoyed many experiences and escapades. Some were friends from schooldays, others were from work, and there were others who, over the years, had become part and parcel of our social life – the kind of friends the children knew as 'uncle' and 'aunt'. We had holidayed together and had been there for each other through some of the most important times of our lives. Now it was all changing. To be fair, they didn't change, I did. With alcohol removed and a new set of life-style values, our former social life didn't hold the same attraction. Now the oft-repeated silly stories of escapades when under the influence of drink brought no smile to my lips but only a deep regret for a life wasted in pursuit of trivia and a sense of shame for the way I had offended God. I think a radical conversion experience generally produces a mixed reaction from friends and family. In my own case, some were sympathetic, some resentful, some confused, and some even offended, but a few recognised that something 'not of this world' had happened and there was no earthly use in fighting it.

Years later I preached a message, which I called the 'Great Divide', based on chapter 6 of Paul's letter to the Galatians. In it I said, ' . . . when we humble ourselves and admit our sin, confessing that we are hell-deserving sinners having no ability to save ourselves, and kneel before the Lord Jesus relying on the cross and trusting in His blood for our salvation, the outcome is that we part company from the world. Paul tells us there are three crucifixions. First, Jesus on the cross. Then, as a result, two other crucifixions take place: the world is crucified to us and the world regards us as crucified. Do you see it my friend? It's in verse 14b of Galatians 6.

Let me make it personal. Before conversion I was anxious to be in agreement and accepted by the world. My goals and aims were set by the world's agenda and I lived, worked and died for the things of the world. But since Jesus came into my life the world has lost its charm. Since my born-again conversion experience the Spirit of God has opened my eyes and allowed me to see this world as God sees it, and I am free from this world of delusion and illusion. I am free from its lies and deceptions, its demands and promises. It's dead to me, crucified. I'm no longer interested in its treasures, its honours or its values. The world preaches a gospel of self: self-fulfilment, self-advancement and selfish pleasures at any cost. But Paul says, 'No, world! I've looked at your wealth. I've seen where your wisdom leads you. I've looked at your vain pride-filled religion and it means nothing. A world whose ethos is to draw men and women away from Jesus has no interest in me, and I have no interest in the world. The world has been crucified to me, and I to the world.'

Paul is in effect saying, 'I judge the world damned, and the world judges me damned, thus we crucify and condemn one another. All that counts is new creation!' (see verse 15). 'It's redemption, reconciliation and restoration, and, world, you know nothing of this. I've seen something and met someone you, world, couldn't even begin to understand. And when He stood before you, unselfish, perfect and filled with love, the best you could do was to nail Him to a cross. So don't try to change my mind, don't waste your breath. Don't try to entice me back into the world. I've seen it and I know it and I am dead to it. Praise God.' Verses from Isaac Watt's hymn 'When I survey the wondrous cross' sum it up for me:

Forbid it, Lord, that I should boast,
Save in the cross of Christ my God:
All the vain things that charm me most,
I sacrifice them to His blood.

Were the whole realm of nature mine,
That were an offering far too small;
Love so amazing, so divine,
Demands my soul, my life, my all!

The reaction from our families was more low-key

*'When I heard it was Hugh playing hymns, I couldn't
believe it! I knew then that he had changed!'*

My mother-in-law told the story of visiting our home and,
when hearing me play hymns on our piano, said, 'When I
heard it was Hugh playing hymns, I couldn't believe it!
I knew then that he had changed!'

There was no hostility or derision from our family, and
though not understanding the full implications, they were
generally happy for us. I think they were all aware of the
problems we were having and thought that whatever it was
that had happened to change me was obviously for the good.

I will always remember my Dad's response when I told
him I had become a Christian. In a bewildered tone he said,
'What do you mean you've become a Christian? You've
always been a Christian, you were in the Boys' Brigade!'

This brought home to me a truth that increasingly I was
to discover. Many men and women in our country today
believe they are 'Christians' because of their backgrounds
or upbringing. For example, having been told a certain

customer attended church, and seeking a kindred spirit, I asked him if he was a Christian. He replied, 'It depends on what you mean by being a Christian.' I said, 'Someone who believes in the virgin birth, the physical crucifixion and bodily resurrection of Jesus, and the Day of Judgment leading to either heaven or hell.' In a slightly shocked tone of voice he said, 'I'm not that sort of Christian!' I explained to him the truth that I was so often to explain in the years ahead, that becoming a Christian is a positive decision one has to make for oneself by confessing sin and accepting Jesus Christ as personal Saviour and Lord. It's theologically wrong and personally very dangerous to be lulled into believing that we become Christians by being born into a Christian family, be they Protestant or Catholic. I often use the term, 'God has no grandchildren', meaning that each one of us has to be born again through a personal encounter with Jesus, and only though His blood can we receive forgiveness of sin. No one else can do this for us or 'pronounce it done!'

With the zeal of the born again we began to evangelise our family and must have often sorely tried their patience. But, as the years passed, one by one they accepted Christ as their Saviour and nineteen years later my sister and then her husband confessed their faith and were baptised in the name of Jesus.

A Sister's Story
Liz Taylor

*God has been good to us and I feel very blessed by Him.
People often think, 'Oh, I would have to stop doing
this or give up the other if I became a Christian.'*

As for me, I had no difficulty whatsoever.
I found I no longer had the desire to do the things I
formally thought were important. Of much more
importance is the peace I've found in the knowledge
that Jesus loves me and is with me always.

How a day can go from calm to chaos! It was a
normal day in July 1997, apart from the fact that I had
an appointment at Ninewells Hospital, Dundee, in
order to have yet another breast lump looked at. I say
it was a normal day because over the previous ten
years I had amassed over one hundred lumps which
had either been aspirated or surgically removed.

I turned up at the clinic as usual and duly saw my
doctor. What was definitely not usual was that after
aspirating four lumps he suggested I should think
about having bilateral surgery. I didn't immediately
grasp what that was, until he went on to talk about
removing the two breasts. It appeared that I was, in
his words, 'a time bomb waiting to go off', and it
had become increasingly difficult for him to know
just what was going on under the surface as these
cysts were very deep. It was explained to me that he
did not normally offer this surgery but in my case
he thought preventative surgery was the way to go!

I kind of sat there numb, nodding my head when
required, and left after an appointment had been
made for me to return to the clinic. During this
time I was to think things over and come to a
decision. I returned to the waiting room where I met
my husband who asked how I had got on. I told him
what my doctor had said, and then followed up with,
'No way. I'm not losing my breasts!' However,

Francis, my husband, took the opposite view and
calmly reasoned the pros and cons of what was
happening. By the end of that night I had come
around to his way of thinking, which was, *better to be
alive and no breasts than to be dead with them!*

I saw the specialist again and it was agreed that I
would have the operation on 13th September.
Because Francis has a heart condition I tried very
hard to be positive and cheery when I was with him,
and also at my work-place. However, when I was
alone I was absolutely petrified. I worried about the
operation, about the anaesthetic and about how I
would cope afterwards.

At that time we were living in Elie, a small fishing
village in the East Neuk of Fife, and every morning I
would take the dog for a walk along the beach before
going to work. It was when I was on these walks
that I had time to be myself and let my thoughts go
wild. I did, however, purely in desperation, start
praying to Jesus. I would like to say that I thought
that praying would be the answer, but I didn't. I was
praying because I couldn't think of anything else to
do that would help me. I continued to pray each
morning, and then all of a sudden one morning when
I was coming back from the beach I realized that I
didn't feel worried any more. I just had this feeling
that everything would be taken care of and that I was
not to worry. This was a funny feeling because at that
time I was the kind of person who would normally
worry if I had nothing to worry about. However, a
strange calmness came over me and I was able to talk
about the operation and think rationally. This
calmness stayed with me – so much so that I think

the people at my work thought I was weird. I worked up until the day before I went into hospital, and on the actual day just before going in for the operation I was shopping in Safeways (now Morrisons) for Francis. In fact, funnily enough, when shopping we met a friend, and he and Francis were having a great discussion about the state of each other's ailments until I suggested that we had to go as I had date with an operating theatre!

The operation went well. When Francis phoned the next morning he couldn't believe it when the nurse told him I was sitting up eating breakfast. This was extremely unusual because any previous time I had had an operation I was always very sick afterwards. He actually told the nurse she must have the wrong person as I was never OK after an operation.

When I went into hospital I took with me a Christian gospel tract that my brother, Hugh, who was a minister, sent me. I had the tract on my bedside locker and every now and then took it down and read it. At this time I would have to say that, although I had been brought up to go to Sunday school and church, I had strayed away and I now realize that I had never really believed in the right way. My thoughts at the time of the operation were more along the lines of, *well it can't do any harm to read it.*

I had the operation and was out of hospital within the week and back at full-time work within three months. I had no great emotions about the removal of my breasts, rather I was just quite relieved that it was all over and I wouldn't have any more lumps.

Part of my good convalescence, I have to say, was
due to my husband's positive attitude towards the
operation. He was really marvellous, and to this day
has never made me feel anything but a whole
woman. Another thing that helped was having a
sense of humour. We quickly learned to joke about
it and even went as far as to 'name' the two
prostheses! (Very odd people?)

Two years passed, and I still felt that somehow I
had changed but still didn't take it further until one
Saturday afternoon an envelope came through the
letterbox. Inside was a lovely hand-painted card with
the words from John 3:16:

*'For God so loved the world, that he gave his only
begotten Son, that whosoever believeth in him should not
perish, but have everlasting life.'*   (KJV)

This really blew me away and I got on the phone to
Hugh. He talked with me, basically assuring me that
I obviously did believe and that I just had to take the
final step and ask Jesus to come into my life. I went
into my room, got down on my knees and prayed
for this. I phoned Hugh and told him what had
happened, telling him that I would go to church on
the following Sunday. At this point I have to say that
Hugh had been praying for me for about nineteen
years. His prayers were indeed answered, albeit in
God's time, not his.

Hugh was not taking any chances. He contacted
the minister of St Andrew's Baptist Church and
asked him if someone from the church fellowship
could come and see me. Two ladies from the church

did come, and Francis and I were there at the church on the Sunday morning. We both subsequently joined the church and were baptised. Our faith has grown through the years.

I can't explain how good it was to be able to be 'on the same wavelength' as my brother and his wife, and we did join them a couple of years ago at the Keswick Convention. We also now have a much better relationship with Francis' family who are nearly all Christians.

God has been good to us in many ways. Francis has had a heart disease for many years and has had three mini-strokes but he is still with us sixteen years on. Recently, when he was diagnosed with bladder cancer, we knew we were not alone in this fight. Francis has faced his illness in the full knowledge that Jesus is with us every step of the way and he has had an amazing spirit every time he has had to have an operation, which is on average every three months. My then future son-in-law was so amazed at the way Francis was coping that he said to me that he didn't think Francis realized how serious his condition was. I assured him that he did but that we were not alone in this fight – we had Jesus, and He would always be there to help us.

I am not saying that life is a bed of roses – far from it – but we know that when we are down we can pray and we get the strength needed to carry on with good spirit. We also have many friends praying for him – from Lincoln, where Hugh and his wife, Joyce, live, up to Aberdeen, where my cousin lives, and lots of places in between. I never doubt the power of prayer now.

God has been good to us and I feel very blessed by Him. People often think, 'Oh, I would have to stop doing this or give up the other if I became a Christian.' As for me, I had no difficulty whatsoever. I found I no longer had the desire to do the things I formally thought were important. Of much more importance is the peace I've found in the knowledge that Jesus loves me and is with me always.

CHAPTER 4

RECOGNISING JESUS AS 'CHAIRMAN' OF THE COMPANY

*The bottom line for me was based on the
rationale that either the Bible is true or it's not.
Either God is who He says He is and can do all the
miraculous things He says He can, or He can't.
If He can't then it's all a waste of time and
I might as well do my own thing.
But if He is the Almighty God revealed in Jesus
Christ that I believed Him to be, then His promises
are true and I cannot lose by trusting Him no
matter how it may look to the contrary or
whatever the outcome may be.*

Following my conversion to Christianity I made a number of decisions that were to have a far-reaching effect upon my life. First, I decided to recognise Jesus as the Chairman of our printing company. This would mean no longer printing any material for the Scotch whisky industry or anything else I considered to be offensive to Jesus. This was a high-risk strategy as the majority of our work came from clients in the alcoholic drink industry. So, to broaden our customer base I decided to actively pursue Christian-based organisations with a view to printing for them. We began an early morning office prayer meeting on Mondays for anyone who wished to attend. We held a Bible study meeting in the factory every Thursday lunch-time led by a local evangelical pastor and gave our employees the opportunity to speak with him if they wished to do so. We employed a number of previously unemployed Christians who were unable to find work (for example, men just out of prison), and endeavoured to establish them and their families in the Christian life. Also, I was not prepared to work on Sundays, which at that time was against Scottish law. I felt that as my family and I were able to benefit from a special day away from the workplace with an opportunity to worship the Lord, then I would not deprive my workforce that same benefit.

I then met with my bank manager who turned grey when I told him about my new business plan. But my thinking was simple: I had given my life to Jesus and entrusted it to Him for all eternity. He certainly could look after my printing company and was able to do a better job than I could. The bottom line for me was based on the rationale that either the Bible is true or it's not. Either God is who He says He is and can do all the miraculous things He says He can, or He can't. If He can't then it's all a waste of time and I might as well do my own thing. But if He is the Almighty God revealed in Jesus Christ that I believed Him to be, then His promises are true and I cannot lose by trusting Him no matter how it may look to the contrary or whatever the outcome may be.

Putting my faith into action I set about returning artwork and film to our customers in the alcoholic drinks trade, explaining that we had stopped supplying this type of work as I believed Satan used alcohol to destroy lives, marriages and families. We also no longer accepted new business of this nature and I confidently expected God to supply new work for our printing presses. He did, and in a miraculous way.

It was mid-afternoon and my sales manager came into the general office and in front of everyone said to me, 'As you know I'm not a Christian, but I have to accept that every time we've turned down orders from the drinks industry another order has come in to replace it.' With everyone's eyes on him, he continued, 'So I have to tell you something big is coming in!'

'What do you mean?' I asked.

He replied, 'This morning we turned down an order for a whisky company's advertising material. Then this afternoon we turned down the order to print a *Clubland* magazine and also refused to quote for a Licensed Trade newspaper.' Looking straight at me he solemnly said, 'Your Chairman [that's Jesus], must have something really big coming in for us, for we have never turned down such a large amount of business before!' There's not much you can say in reply to that and amidst friendly laughter of the 'I wish' variety, he left the office.

Later that evening when the office staff had gone home, a very large articulated vehicle drew up outside our premises. The driver came in and told me he had thirty tons of paper for me. I laughed, as I told him, 'I have never ordered thirty tons of paper in my life.' To which he replied, 'You better have. There are two more truckloads on the way. I'm the first of three; we left Holland last night with one hundred tons of paper for your address. The other two trucks will be here in the morning.' I had no idea what was going on and told him that a mistake must have been made and suggested he settle down for the night in our loading bay and we would sort it all out in the morning.

While walking back to my office my telephone began to ring. On the line was a senior production manager from the manufacturing plant of a large multinational publishing concern located very close to my small company. He told me that they had experienced a production line problem and, desperately needing help, had diverted one hundred tons of their paper to my premises. He wanted us to print a series of books and manuals for them and would I please, please, call in to his office in the morning and pick up the job specifications and orders.

That evening I telephoned my sales manager at his home and said, 'Remember your comments this morning? Just wait and see what the "Chairman" has in store for you tomorrow!' The following day we collected the official orders and specifications to print one hundred tons of books and manuals. Praise God!

You may call it coincidence if you like, but bearing in mind the public comments made by the non-believing sales manager that we could expect something really big from God because of the business we had refused, I knew this was a special gift from God. The Red Sea parts and a nation is saved. Water turns to wine and a wedding is saved. Loaves and fishes multiply and a public picnic is saved. A production line has a problem and a small printing company is saved. And the most wonderful thing of all was that I had done nothing to earn it: it came directly from the hand of God.

The following promise was made famous in the film *Chariots of Fire* and comes from 1 Samuel 2:30:

> 'The LORD, the God of Israel, declares: . . . "Those who honour me I will honour . . . " '

I was about to discover there was much more to all this than met the eye. The books we were to print were computer manuals and the whole project was cloaked with secrecy; so much so that it even had a code name. It turned out that the then world's largest computer manufacturer, IBM, was about to begin production of a new product called the PC at its manufacturing plant in Scotland. The multinational publishing company had the contract to print all the manuals for the computers and those of you who recall early computer manuals will understand how big this project was. The one hundred tons of paper was for a trial run of non-English language computer manuals. We supplied these books and as we met the high quality control and price requirements, we subsequently secured the subcontract to print all the computer manuals in foreign languages for Europe and the Middle East. It was a massive undertaking: easily the largest print order currently being placed in Scotland. It meant full production and to meet the demand we started six-day, twenty-four hour, continuous shift working. Everyone was happy.

We had been going full blast for several months when something very significant happened that was to teach me a valuable lesson: one that would stand me in good stead in the years to come.

I was asked to attend an important meeting hosted at director level by our now very important customer. Accompanying me was my production director who knew all the quality specifications and delivery schedules for the manuals we were printing. The setting was a caricature of a high-level meeting. A rather short man with a large cigar, sitting behind a huge oak desk, told us he had good news and bad news. The good news was that the new product (the PC) was selling like 'hot-cakes': the bad news was that I needed to increase production significantly to meet the huge demand and I had to do it fast.

I replied that I was very pleased everything was going well, but as we were already working twenty-four hours for six days a week, there was no way we could increase production quickly: it would mean a larger factory, more machinery and an increase in the workforce.

I will never forget the baffled expression on my customer's face as he exclaimed, 'What do you mean six days, there are seven days in the week!'

I felt a sinking feeling and thought, 'Oh, no!'

The voice from behind the cigar smoke cut across the silence of the room, 'Are you working Sundays?'

In the Old Testament Book of Nehemiah, it's recorded that Nehemiah wanted to leave the king's service in Persia and return to help rebuild the ruined walls of Jerusalem. Burdened by the thought of his suffering countrymen, his face was sober in the king's presence. Noticing this, the king asked Nehemiah what was wrong with him. Before answering the king Nehemiah prayed to the God of heaven (see Nehemiah 2:4). This has become known as an 'arrow prayer'; that is, a short, sharp prayer for help directed

upwards! This is what I did when confronted with the
question about Sunday working: 'Please God! Help me!'

I told the director and the others in his office that I was a
born-again Christian and did not believe it was right to
work unnecessarily on Sundays. I said that I realized there
were important tasks that were necessary to carry out on
Sundays, but unfortunately printing his manuals was not
one of them! You could have cut the atmosphere with a
knife. From behind the cigar smoke the voice said, 'You do
understand that this is one of the biggest print contracts
going in Scotland and there are a number of companies
who want it?'

I said, 'I do understand that, and I also realize that you
have to do that which is right for you and your customer,
but under no circumstances are we printing on Sundays.'

The meeting was adjourned and we were out in the car
park. My production director was ashen-faced and said to
me, 'We're finished!'

I replied, 'No we're not.' I told my colleague, 'I may only
have been a Christian for eighteen months or so, but I have
read the Book of Job, and recall Job saying, *'the LORD gave,
and the LORD hath taken away; blessed be the name of the LORD'*
(Job 1:21 KJV). I said, 'Remember how we got this contract?
We didn't fight for it, or win it, it was given to us. It started
with a hundred tons of paper turning up on our doorstep!
The Lord gave it to us, and no-one, but no-one, can take it
from us unless He says so, and if He is allowing it to go, I
will trust Him for another one.'

My colleague, although not professing faith in Christ
said, 'I will go along with you.'

The Christians in our work-place prayed, others bit their
finger nails for a few agonising days, then I received a
phone call from the cigar-smoking director who said, 'Go

ahead and buy your new machinery and hire your extra workers, we are increasing the order with you by 100%.' Praise God! So, I bought more printing and finishing machinery and doubled the number of our employees, and all this on top of our normal quality print business from a wide variety of sources. We truly were being blessed.

CHAPTER 5

OUR NEW MARRIAGE AND FAMILY LIFE

*I was beginning to discover that when you decide
to follow Jesus you do not always know where that
decision will take you, how much it will cost you,
and the extent to which it will change you.*

The blessing, of course, was not restricted to our business. With alcohol no longer in the picture, our marriage and family life changed out of all recognition. The church where we made our spiritual home, now known as Greenview Evangelical Church, on the south side of Glasgow, was absolutely wonderful. The folk there were warm and welcoming, and went out of their way to integrate our family into the Christian life. It was here that my wife and I were baptised along with our daughter Jacqui, and I can still remember the apprehensive expressions of my many non-Christian friends who were invited to the baptismal service they were anxious in case what had happened to me happened to them!

As a family we began to attend an All-Age Bible Class before the Sunday morning worship service. Our obvious hunger for knowledge of Christianity was met by mature Christian men and women who spent quality time teaching us Christian doctrine as well as being a tremendous source of encouragement to us.

We were voraciously reading Christian books. I can recall the first time our family went into a Christian bookshop to buy Bibles. The shop was situated in the centre of Glasgow and never once in forty-two years had I ventured inside. It was a foreign land to me. Now there we were buying five Bibles: one for each of us. Then off home to read and share precious quotes and promises from the pages of Scripture. We then began to meet each morning for Bible study and family prayers, and this became so much part of my new life that the habit has never left me.

I still treasure some precious memories from that time. My son, then aged about twelve, gave thanks to God for 'what He had done in the past, what He was doing now, and what He would do in the future'. I have often prayed that prayer since and always think back to those early pre-breakfast family gatherings.

It's hard to describe the difference living to a completely new agenda brought to my life. Each day I would learn something new that reinforced the change that was taking place within me. Let me give you some examples.

I had to attend two funerals within a day of each other.

The first was for an aunt who, like most of the family, professed no faith in Christ. The service and committal was 'cold', especially when the mourners tried to sing the 23rd Psalm – 'The Lord's My Shepherd'. As none of them knew the 'Shepherd' and had absolutely no understanding of what would happen when it was their time to walk through the 'Valley of the Shadow of Death', the singing was mumbled and embarrassing. The following day's funeral service was for a man of strong Christian faith who had been a stalwart member of my new church. The building was packed to capacity and believing friends and family sang great and glorious hymns of praise and thanksgiving with the assurance that the one they knew and loved was safe in the arms of Jesus.

I'm not sure if there is a better way of seeing the difference between believers and non-believers than in their behaviour at a funeral service. For one group, warm-hearted testimony about the deceased gives way to the Christian belief that death marks the beginning of a new life in the company of Jesus with all the glorious promises He gave concerning it. That being the case, a Christian funeral always looks back with thanks for the life of the deceased and then forward to his or her promise of glory. For the others, yes, warm testimony is often given and happy memories relived, but generally no mention is ever made of the future of the deceased because for many the future after death is a dark, dreadful unknown.

Another example of the changes in our family concerned our annual holiday that year. We had previously arranged to spend two weeks in France after driving south from Scotland via the Channel car ferry. When the holiday was originally planned my wife was concerned that it would become an alcoholic trip through the vineyards of France.

But with alcohol removed from our agenda we enjoyed a marvellous family holiday.

On our return home there was the threat of a ferry strike, so to avoid it we caught an earlier crossing arriving at the south coast of England in the evening and began to drive north. Around 10 o'clock, when we were all tired and grubby from travelling, a late-evening mist began to descend making driving difficult, and I realized that we would have to stop and find somewhere to spend the night. But where? Explaining the situation to the family I asked them to pray. Within seconds of them doing so, a Travelodge sign loomed out of the mist and I drove to the reception.

Explaining our need, I was told that they were holding a large family room against a reservation, but as it was now 10.00 pm and the reservation was only valid until 8.00 pm, we were welcome to have the room. A very grateful, tired and dirty Hill family rejoiced at the prospect of hot water, large clean towels, coffee, and a good night's sleep. To our surprise and delight the following morning we discovered a filling breakfast was included in the price and we thanked the Lord for His goodness to us before driving home rejoicing.

On many occasions I was faced with entering the unknown, but I knew within myself I had everything to gain by pressing on and not holding back. So, when I was asked to pray publicly, answer a biblical question, or give my testimony, I did so. Though painfully aware of my lack of experience, time after time I found God was there for me. I began to learn that when you become a Christian and consciously make the prayerful decision to move on in your faith, you have to be willing to leave your comfort zone, to be prepared to discard your preconceived notions of how you would do things and accept that challenges are designed to make you strong. I was learning that, while we all enjoy the mountain-top experiences, nothing grows on mountain-tops; growth is in the valley below. And sometimes God has to take us by the hand and lead us down into the dark valley depths where we will be receptive to His teaching and training. I was beginning to discover that when you decide to follow Jesus you do not always know where that decision will take you, how much it will cost you, and the extent to which it will change you. As Christians we ask the Lord to use us for His glory; we can't hedge that prayer with conditions – it's all or nothing.

CHAPTER 6

Towards Christian Literature

I had been a Christian for only a relatively short time and had now learned a vital lesson that would stay with me throughout my Christian life: nothing, but nothing, is impossible for God.

My ambition to enhance the kingdom of God became a burning desire and in the autumn of 1982 I had a new idea: that our printing company should move into the production of Christian books and literature. By doing so, we could assist mission organisations by supplying them with their print requirements at very competitive prices. To achieve this would mean the purchase of a new printing press and allied binding machinery, but the larger and more efficient printing press and machinery would enable us to produce our present workload more efficiently and become more competitive. In addition, our profit margin would increase and we would be able to break into high-volume markets. The downside was that our finances were precarious and we did not have any large customers in the Christian publishing sector. Now was not the time to embark on this enterprise, and my senior management made that point quite clearly and forcefully.

I was now faced with a question: as a relatively young Christian wanting to serve the Lord, what should I do when I wasn't sure of the way forward? To try to find an answer, I turned to Scripture.

In verse 1 of 1 Samuel 14, King Saul's son, Jonathan, planned to attack a fortified Philistine position. Reading on, we find that Jonathan and his armour-bearer were heavily outnumbered and, wanting to make sure the Lord was with him in order to gain victory, we are told:

> 'Jonathan said, "Come, then; we will cross over towards the men and let them see us. If they say to us, 'Wait there until we come to you,' we will stay where we are and not go up to them. But if they say, 'Come up to us,' we will climb up, because that will be our sign that the LORD has given them into our hands'"'   (1 Samuel 14:8–10)

The Philistine soldiers then did invite the two Israelites to come up so they could teach them a lesson and Jonathan, taking that as his 'green light' from God, climbed up the hill and overwhelmed the enemy.

This practice, of seeking a tangible sign from the Lord in order to have His approval to make an important decision is known as 'putting out a fleece'. It was most famously recorded in chapter 6 of the Book of Judges. On that occasion God told the young Gideon that he would become a mighty warrior and deliver the nation of Israel from enemy occupation. From Gideon's perspective this seemed impossible to achieve. But rather than show lack of faith and refuse to believe God, verses 36–40 record how Gideon put out a fleece and asked God for a clear sign that he could see with his own eyes. Gideon needed the personal assurance that God was with him and that whatever was happening wasn't due to his imagination or wishful thinking. God miraculously answered his request and Gideon obediently followed His instructions. Through a series of amazing incidents he became a mighty warrior and liberated Israel.

Applying this biblical precedent to my own situation and wanting to please God, I followed the example of Jonathan and Gideon and put out my 'fleece'.

I asked my senior management, 'What would you want to see God do as a sign for us to go ahead and commit to purchase a larger printing press and binding equipment in order to move into large-volume Christian printing?'

Their answer was unanimous and unequivocal, 'First, by the end of the year the overdraft must be zero and, secondly, a stranger must ask us to print a Christian book.'

That brought derisory laughter of the 'there's no way' variety – especially the thought of the overdraft going down to zero. With our critical cash flow there was absolutely no way that was possible. My colleagues thought they were on to a sure thing and, to be honest, I was inclined to agree with them. Nevertheless, I took this proposal before the Lord in prayer and promised that if by some miracle the overdraft reached zero by the end of the year and a stranger appeared asking us to print a Christian book, we would buy the machinery and begin to help Christian organisations. I then told my colleagues what I had done and said that no matter how impossible these requirements may appear now, when they happened we had better be ready to respond positively.

As the summer months passed, our financial dilemma intensified. Business was booming but the cash flow to support it was an ongoing problem. Then, unbelievably, the bank started to make unreasonable demands insisting that our overdraft be eliminated. It all seemed so unfair; there we were with the largest commercial print contract in Scotland for two rock-solid 'blue chip' organisations and the bank manager was acting like an adversary. With the enormous burden of financial constraints placed upon us and the factory working at full capacity, all thoughts of the 'fleece' faded from our minds. Determined to trade our way out of our financial difficulties we were in survival mode.

In the autumn of that year, under intense financial pressure, we were visited by an executive from a finance company who introduced himself with the words, 'I may be able to help you.' He represented a highly-respected national financial organisation involved with factoring company debts. We entered into negotiations and our financial advisers and accountants gave me the green light to proceed. The outcome was that in November we received a very substantial cheque for most of the money we were owed by our customers. This radically transformed our position with the bank for the better.

As our financial situation began to improve it dawned on me that this last crisis and unexpected outcome had all the appearance of the Lord working towards the 'fleece' being honoured. Then, one afternoon, a visitor arrived at our reception and introduced himself as the secretary of the Mission to Military Garrisons, a long-established Christian organisation involved in running hospitality centres in military garrisons around the world. It was their centenary and having heard that I was a Christian, he asked if we were interested in printing their centennial book. A stranger had arrived and asked us to print a Christian book: clearly the second part of the fleece had been fulfilled.

The month of December saw a steady decline in the overdraft and, at the end of the year, after receiving a huge payment of money owed to us, the overdraft was zero. God had answered the 'impossible' fleece. I had been a Christian for only a relatively short time and had now learned a vital lesson that would stay with me throughout my Christian life: nothing, but nothing, is impossible for God.

I've often been asked if I think it's right to 'put out a fleece' today since we now have the New Testament which gives clearer teaching on Christian guidance. In reply, I would say that there is a danger of using the 'fleece' instead of prayer, Bible study and Christian counsel. However, if having exhausted the normal means of biblical guidance and your motive is to genuinely serve the Lord, and you believe you are facing a complex course of action in which the wrong decision has the potential to cause harm to others or bring dishonour to God's name, then, yes, I believe that it is quite acceptable to ask God for a sign of His approval. However, it should be carefully borne in mind that the use of a fleece may lead to your faith being tested: if the sign is answered positively you must proceed obediently. You can hardly ask God to give you a clear sign for your personal guidance and then refuse to proceed obediently when the sign is clearly given. So, be very, very careful about entering into a 'fleece' and think carefully about what you ask for. Remember, too, that God never ever contradicts plain Scripture teaching.

Our company directors and senior management all agreed to fulfil our side of the understanding and early in 1983 I purchased the book printing and binding machinery for our new venture and moved our manufacturing focus to that area of business.

Still a relatively new Christian, I had learned the old adage, 'When I pray, coincidences happen', and through a remarkable series of unexpected phone calls from people with machinery for sale our plans began to fall into place.

Another lesson all Christians need to learn is that we walk by faith, and that God frequently tests our faith to develop and refine us.

In February we were awaiting the delivery of the very large printing press which would print both sides of an A0 size sheet of paper; that is, thirty-two pages of A4 on one pass through the machine. I well remember being told by senior management at a production meeting that, 'We have nothing to print on this machine when it is installed.' The inference being, 'It's too big and a waste of money!' However, I had no doubt that this was God's plan and trusted Him to provide the necessary work.

This coincided with me undertaking to print material for a Christian organisation as a gift to them, and my statement to God that I trusted Him and would live up to my side of the 'fleece'. While I was confident that God would honour His promise, the timing of the 'gift' was unhelpful as our sales forecast for that quarter was particularly low and the 'gift' would adversely affect our ever-present cash flow difficulties. When the order for the Christian organisation was completed I was absolutely overjoyed to be told that we had just received an unexpected enormous order for a re-run of computer manuals with a required delivery date of 'yesterday'. Since we had previously printed the manuals we had standing printing plates and could commence production as soon as the paper arrived. I smiled broadly when my production people asked if I could speed up the delivery and installation of the new giant printing press as they would need it to fulfil this new order. Some people may call this 'coincidence'; to me it was an obvious confirmation from God. Thank You, Lord.

Now with around sixty employees, the new continuous shift system, and increased machine capacity, our output was substantially enlarged and the year continued with us developing new skills and expertise in the area of book production. As a rising number of Christian publishers and para-church organisations approached us with their print requirements, there was a sense of excitement and buoyancy as more and more Christian literature was printed. At this time I contacted a major Christian publisher and secured orders for two large volume paperback books for distribution in the USA and UK.

The extra wage costs arising from the new shift system plus the expenditure for the new printing and binding machinery meant an ongoing strain on cash flow but happily, as the year came to a close, our accountants were pleased to announce a profit from our trial balance sheet. While that was very gratifying, so, too, was the fact that the year ended with us printing one-and-a-half million full-colour booklets in twenty-nine different languages entitled *Christ Is the Answer*, as well as several thousand copies of the New Testament in the Czechoslovakian language, two Bible commentary books and numerous pamphlets and leaflets for Bible societies and missionary organisations. All told, this was incredibly satisfying.

I had agreed to supply a print order for five thousand New Testaments in the Mongolian language. Being under communist domination at that time there was no known Christian church in Mongolia and the Bibles were to be smuggled into Mongolia by Brother Andrew's organisation, Open Doors. A young Dutch Christian arrived at our factory having travelled over from Holland with the film from which we would make printing plates. I mentioned to him that I was excited about this project, and he replied that he felt the same way. 'In fact,' he said, 'while crossing the North Sea last night I told the Lord that I was very eager about this whole assignment. I then sensed the Lord say to me that the day would come when we would be in glory, and the Lord would take us by the hand and introduce us to a Mongolian family who were there as a direct result of reading His Word in their native tongue!' Wow! You don't get that reaction from every print order.

There's a rather wonderful postscript to this story. On Good Friday, 2006, I was preaching in the Christian Community Church in Kabul, Afghanistan. Aware of the international nature of the congregation, I repeated the story above regarding the Mongolian New Testaments, adding some particular details about the nature of the translation. At the end of the service I was approached by an Englishman who said to me, 'You will not have to wait till you get to glory, brother,' and he introduced me to a Mongolian lady who had become a Christian by reading a New Testament we had printed twenty years previously in Scotland. Isn't God good?

The pressure of running a fast-expanding printing company took much of my time and attention but I continued

to attend church twice on Sunday, a mid-week Bible study /
prayer meeting and an early Saturday morning prayer
meeting on a regular basis. I remember talking to someone
who said they had tried Christianity but 'hadn't got much
from it', and I recognised they had received exactly what
they had put into it – which wasn't a lot. I know it sounds
unspiritual but God is no man's debtor. You simply cannot
reach a position where God owes you. The more you give
to Him the more He blesses you. To repeat the famous
promise from God: *'Those who honour me I will honour'*
(1 Samuel 2:30).

I determined to honour God with my time, money and
business, and to trust Him for the future. It wasn't as
ridiculous as it sounds when you consider what the
situation had been around eighteen months previously.
Now our marriage and family life were being richly blessed
as my life was no longer self-centred but God-centred. I was
increasingly being invited to speak at evangelistic dinners
and church events to tell those present how I became a
Christian. Significantly, I and others sensed that God was
working through me and this was confirmed when telephone calls were received from men and women affected
by my message, and from some who had given their lives
to Christ. This caused me to think about the possibility of
full-time ministry in the future but my limited experience as
a practising Christian, plus my heavy commitment to our
business, seemed to bar any progress in that direction.

Since becoming a Christian family, we had already
received and thanked God for many answers to prayer as
well as experiencing many personal touches from God on
our lives. Here are a few examples.

First, one of Jacqui's close friends became a Christian
during the Christmas of 1983, not only giving cause for

rejoicing but also providing a terrific boost to Jacqui's faith. Then, aged between fifteen and sixteen, Jacqui wanted to meet some new Christian friends and broaden her horizons. So, we prayed that God would lead her into new opportunities to serve Him. Shortly afterwards in the spring of 1984 she was invited to join the Christian singing group New Horizon, which was particularly popular in West of Scotland church circles. Jacqui then prayed that at her first concert someone would become a Christian, and God graciously answered her prayer.

Secondly, twelve-year-old Jonathan had set his heart on becoming a pilot and in our family prayer time asked the Lord to help him in this direction. A few weeks later I had the privilege of helping a Christian organisation, and by way of thanks their company secretary offered to help me in any way he could. When I asked him what sort of help he had in mind, he said, 'I own a light aeroplane, if ever that could be of help . . . ' So, a week later Jon held the controls of a light plane as we flew over the Clyde estuary.

Thirdly, we experienced God's personal touch on our lives during a significant week of our family holiday in 1983 at the Keswick Convention. It's hard to explain the powerful impact this had on all of us. In the company of two thousand or so Bible-believing Christians we listened to God's Word being explained and applied. Then, each afternoon as a family, we enjoyed the Lakeland hills which were a special blessing. At the time, I was reading a book on the life of King David, called *The Making of a Man of God* by Alan Redpath. I was thoroughly enjoying the book and learning much from it, so I was delighted to discover that the main speaker for the week was none other than Alan Redpath.

Now I know these examples may not sound particularly impressive to you, the reader but, together with many others, these very personal touches of God's hand in our lives were a continual source of comfort and encouragement to us, and were strategic in strengthening our faith for what lay ahead.

WORTHING
HONOUR
TRUST
LOVE
HOLY BIBLE
GLASGOW

CHAPTER 7

THE BATTLE BELONGS TO THE LORD

Each of us can achieve far more than we realize by living out our Christian faith in front of the watching eyes of friends and family.

The way the New Year began in 1984 illustrated the change in our lives. We hosted a church party in our home, enjoying laughter, friendship and good food. At midnight as the clock ushered in the New Year we read Scripture and prayed, thanking God for the year past and committing ourselves to Him for the coming year. I was drawn to verse 1a of Isaiah 56 with its instruction to '*maintain justice and do what is right*'.

This attitude of faithful commitment was carried over into our workplace as a number of us who were Christians met for prayer in our office at 7.30 am on the first working day of the New Year. One of our group spoke about a Scripture passage that he felt had special significance for us. It was from 2 Chronicles 20, which tells the story of King Jehoshaphat in Jerusalem being threatened by an advancing, overwhelming enemy force. Jehoshaphat went before the Lord in prayer seeking His help and received the assurance, '*Do not be afraid or discouraged because of this vast army. For the battle is not yours, but God's*' (2 Chronicles 20:15). Sure enough, when Jehoshaphat and his army went out to fight, to their joy they discovered their enemy had been destroyed by fighting among themselves. As if in confirmation, Joyce and I had also been impressed by verses 1–5 of Isaiah 43 where God promises to be with us when we go through flood and fire. We took particular comfort from the fact that we are not spared the dangers but promised God's presence with us through them. So we went into the New Year conscious that it was highly likely that we were going to have great opportunities, yet face many challenges. We were not mistaken: our faith would indeed be tested. But first, a matter of rejoicing.

One of my managers had come to faith in Jesus and he and his wife were baptised in the Baptist church they attended. Their baptismal service was quite wonderful and a number of our workforce were present for the occasion. There was a sense of the Lord's presence among joyful worshipping Christians. The event was especially pleasing for me, because when I came became a born-again Christian, I had spoken about the Lord Jesus to this manager but had been told in no uncertain manner that he didn't want to hear what I had to say. He had made it perfectly clear that although he worked for me, he did not have to listen to my Christian viewpoint. Of course, he was right. I took it to heart and refrained from approaching him again on the subject of Christianity. But now, there we were with cups of tea in hand talking together after his baptism. I reminded him of our previous conversation and asked what had made him change his mind. He said, 'Watching you. I knew what you had been and saw the change in your life. As time passed I could not ignore the reality of what I saw. I had to take your claim seriously.' That night I learned the importance of the Christian's 'silent witness'. Each of us can achieve far more than we realize by living out our Christian faith in front of the watching eyes of friends and family.

Then came some disastrous news. Our largest customer informed us that we had lost the contract for the computer manuals. This contract was the basis for our twenty-four-hour shift system, as well as the extra machinery and staff. Withdrawal of such a large amount of turnover threatened the existence of our company. I was very concerned. We needed help from the Lord.

At that time we had about fifteen Christians in our workforce and I called a prayer meeting to bring the matter before the Lord. We thanked Him for what He had been doing in and through our company, for the men and women who had become Christians, for the millions of pieces of gospel literature that had been sent out to dozens of countries, for the many opportunities we had been given to honour Him, and then asked Him to take this matter into His hands and do as He saw fit.

Following this I had a visit from one of our trade union shop stewards. Remember, I did not own a Christian printing company; it was a secular company in which the majority of the workforce were non-believers and were represented by three militant trade unions.

The shop steward who spoke to me on behalf of the entire workforce was a professing communist. I smile now when I think how a new generation of young people are growing up in our country today who don't know anything about communism. It's quite wonderful how communism has been discredited and vanquished. It's proof of the way that all man-made anti-God creeds and philosophies ultimately come to nothing while the truth of Jesus Christ marches on from strength to strength.

The spokesman said that he had heard we had lost the 'big order', and as I nodded agreement he asked what I was going to do about it. I told him that I had already taken action, explaining that a number of us had taken the matter before the Lord Jesus Christ in prayer and were leaving it with Him to sort out. He looked at me as if I was mad and said, 'But I'm serious. What are you really going to do?' I replied that I, too, was serious.

I've often thought of that encounter, for it sums up for me the gulf between the Christian believer and the non-believer. You see, two years previously I would have felt broadly similar to the way that he did. Not that I believed in communism, but in the secular belief that we can trust only in our own strength and goodness and that of other men and women to face life's difficulties. The historic downfall of communism and the shocking revelations regarding the hundreds of millions of innocent people killed by Stalin and Mao more than prove the fallacy of this secular argument. It's also worth noting that if you include Hitler with Stalin and Mao you have the three men collectively responsible for the greatest number of innocent deaths in history, which is a powerful argument against those who blame religion for the world's wars.

Contrary to this secular belief, I was facing this latest difficulty by placing my trust in a Person far wiser and stronger than myself. My faith was in God's ability not mine. I was under no illusions concerning my weakness, but equally I had no doubts concerning the power and ability of God. So, yes, it may sound simplistic for me to have said to the scornful communist that, 'I've done all that's necessary and brought the problem to the attention of the Lord,' but the bottom line for me was that it was true and I rested my case on that statement of faith.

We now embarked upon a desperate attempt to make up for the loss of the contract. We redoubled our sales efforts and a number of really solid potential possibilities opened up. But the reality was that with such a gigantic hole in our sales forecasts only the Lord could save us. The mood was not good. The fact that we had lost the big order was the current gossip of the printing trade and did nothing to raise our spirits.

In the midst of all this anxiety, I received a phone call from the local newspaper asking if they could do a face-to-face interview. The journalist explained that they had heard of my conversion to Christianity and the dramatic changes in our company and wanted to do a story about it. I thought, 'How typical that this invitation should happen at such an awful time as this.' As I hesitated, my mind went back to our text at the start of the year about Jehoshaphat and the battle belonging to the Lord. I realized that it's one thing to be interviewed after the victory, when the bodies are lying in the valley, and give glory to the Lord for the victory. But now? At this dark and difficult time everything within me shrank from publicity of this nature. However, I agreed to go ahead with the interview, sensing the Lord was saying, 'Yes I hear your prayers. Now let Me see you put your words of faith to the world into action!' In my heart of hearts I hoped that the interview would be some undetermined time in the future, but the journalist asked if he could visit my office that same afternoon. With a sinking feeling in my stomach I said, yes!

Later that morning, I took a significant phone call from a very senior executive of the large organisation for whom we had printed the computer manuals. He intimated that they were having another look at their future requirements and were mindful of our high quality, excellent service, competitive price and the expertise we had acquired. He added they would take all that into consideration as they assessed their future needs. It was, to say the least, hopeful.

Then our sales manager arrived at the office to announce we had just won a major contract for the Sinclair Spectrum computer manuals. While not as big as the contract we had lost, it was, nevertheless, very substantial and absolutely wonderful news at a time when we were quite apprehensive about the future, and we all rejoiced.

The following day we had convened a board meeting and as we gathered together we were interrupted with the quite incredible news that the original contract for computer manuals that we had lost had been renewed and the new orders were to be collected from our customer's office that afternoon. So there we were, with more business than ever and every ounce of spare capacity taken up. Isn't God good? Whoever said the Christian life was boring?

What with newspaper articles about the boss's Christian faith and all the other incredible things that were happening, our workforce could not help but be aware of the marked change in our company. A number of their colleagues were regularly participating in our Bible studies and attending church services, which resulted in more and more of them having meaningful discussions with Christians in the workforce. I was visiting one family at their home to lead them in a Bible study, and they too became Christians.

On the Thursday of that eventful week I had been asked to speak at the lunch-time Bible study that was held in our office. I still remember walking through to the office where about ten or twelve people usually met, only to be redirected to another larger room where forty people were gathered for the study. It was an incredible surprise, but thrilling. I sat down, opened the meeting in prayer and began my prepared study. I based the study on several passages of Scripture that had been a source of encouragement to us as we faced the challenge and difficulties of the past few weeks. First, I pointed out that when Job was under great pressure, he nevertheless proclaimed, '*the* LORD *gave, and the* LORD *hath taken away; blessed be the name of the* LORD' (Job 1:21 KJV), and we had learnt a lesson from that. Secondly, I explained how 2 Chronicles 20 had been a source of encouragement to us. Thirdly, I drew attention to God's promises to us from Jeremiah 29:11 and after looking at some of the claims of Jesus in John chapter 6, I concluded with a challenge using a question from Jesus to His disciples, '*Who do you say I am?*' (Matthew 16:15).

So, by April 1984, exactly two years from the time when I became a born-again Christian, my life and printing company were unrecognisable. We owed the bank nothing, PAYE was up to date, a VAT repayment was owing to us, the order book was full for the foreseeable future, and we were producing an enormous variety of Christian books and literature. I have to stress that it was not easy and cash flow

was a constant headache. The bank often seemed to be
working against the best interests of the company and
workforce. In addition, there was the constant pressure to
meet quality standards and delivery schedules, but despite
all these difficulties we managed to maintain the necessary
profit margin to enable the company to survive.

CHAPTER 8

COINCIDENCES OR GOD-INCIDENTS?

*We either have faith in God and His overruling
ability to perform wonder-working miracles,
or we dismiss the evidence as coincidence and in so
doing put our lives further and further away from
the influence and person of Jesus Christ.
So, I suggest there's either a will to believe or a will
not to believe. The outworking of the choice we
make will either draw us closer to God,
or drive us further away from Him.*

My sales manager told me that he could not ignore the
miraculous events he had witnessed while working for our

company. He had attended our lunch-time office Bible studies and had conversations concerning things of Christ with other believers. He said had begun to pray and attend his local church and felt he was near to accepting Jesus Christ as his Saviour.

Just after that conversation I was invited to speak to a number of young Christians in their teens and early twenties at a Christian centre in Linlithgow. They were soon to go on summer mission with a Scottish evangelistic organisation. My date to speak a message of encouragement to them was a Saturday slightly less than two weeks ahead.

Over recent months I had received orders to print several thousand copies each of six Christian paperback books from a publisher in the south. While I had hoped this would lead to something significant, I was not particularly optimistic, as for a variety of reasons the quality of our work had been less than our normal high standard and our delivery had been late. So, as I was driving south on the M6 to meet with the publisher that evening I felt I was wasting my time, money, and effort. To add to my unease, I had been invited to stay overnight at the home of the managing director of the publishing company, and I was conscious that if understandably they complained about our poor service, my visit could be embarrassing for all concerned. I even considered declining the invitation and staying in a hotel for the night.

Such was my frame of mind as I drove southwards from Scotland. Then, unusually for me, I began to feel quite unwell. So much so that I wondered whether I should return home. Sensing that all was not as it should be and that the problem may be spiritual, I began a long conversation with the Lord. As I unburdened myself and talked with God, an idea came into my mind: it would make a lot of sense if my company printing Christian literature in the north could work closely with the Christian publisher in the south – perhaps even with the two companies becoming financially involved.

It seemed a logical development, but as I spoke to God I wasn't at all sure where that thought came from. Was the devil leading me into some dream of vain glory, or was it the Lord guiding me into a new, exciting future for His purposes? So, I prayed again, specifically asking, 'Is this You, Lord, or is it the devil?' I sensed the Lord saying that it was Him and everything was going to work out. I was to continue the journey and trust Him.

Having learned not to rely on feelings, I said, 'But, Lord, how do I know it's You and not the enemy deceiving me?' The reply came clearly into my mind: 'Next Thursday at the lunch-time Bible study your sales manager [God used his first name] will accept Jesus as his Saviour and on the following Saturday when you speak to the young people at Linlithgow you will tell them this story including the outcome yet to happen.'

By this time I was on the M5 south of Birmingham and the Lord had told me three things: (1) this trip was going to be very worthwhile, (2) my sales manager would become a Christian next Thursday, and (3) I would have something really encouraging to tell the young people next Saturday.

I did the only thing possible; I continued my journey south and in the early evening arrived at the home of the managing director of the publishing company. He and his wife were waiting for me with smiles and a warm welcome.

It was a beautiful sunny evening and dinner was served in the garden. Over coffee the three of us talked over our recent production problems and resolved them quite amicably. The publisher then produced orders for another five paperback books and in addition asked me to provide prices for manufacturing a range of thirty paperback book titles for the UK and USA markets with quantities of up to 50,000 each. I was also offered a position as a trustee of the Christian publishing company in the UK and a directorship of the American publishing division. We would print all the publisher's books for the US market as well as for the UK and they would take a stock holding in our printing company. That evening before going to sleep I thanked the Lord for His goodness, and recalled Proverbs 3:5–6:

> 'Trust in the LORD with all your heart
>   and lean not on your own understanding;
> in all your ways acknowledge him,
>   and he will make your paths straight.'

Life is certainly exciting when we trust God, isn't it?

Upon my return to Glasgow I called a board meeting and our directors gave their unanimous consent to the proposals. We negotiated a new structure for additional directors and shareholders and at this point in time I put my home up as collateral for the increased bank loan required. We also realized we needed more production space and were aware that there was an empty 50,000 sq. ft factory next to our present premises that would be ideal for our requirements. After much consultation with our production management we agreed to move from our present factory into the larger one.

Obviously, the following days and nights were filled with activity: meetings, cash flow projections, production requirements and a hundred-and-one important decisions that needed to be made. I am ashamed to confess that I completely forgot about the promise from God for the office

Bible study, and it was not until during my personal quiet time early on the Thursday morning that I remembered it. I said to the Lord, 'Lord, it's today You said a "certain person" will become a Christian!'

During the morning with all the sales and production activity the promise again went completely out of my mind until lunch-time arrived and I was reminded that it was time for the Bible study group. It was well attended and afterwards my sales manager quietly approached me and said he wanted to become a Christian. For privacy, we went out to my car and sitting there we prayed and I led him to the Lord Jesus.

The following Saturday at Linlithgow I found myself about to speak to thirty or so young evangelists. I said to them, 'I have to tell you a story . . . ' and proceeded to give them my testimony bringing it right up to date by including the events of the past two weeks. Everything that I had prayed for and received confirmation about had literally happened.

I really don't think we can logically write off these incidents as a chain of coincidences. Not only was each of these events totally unexpected, but the fact that they were forecast to happen moves the whole episode into a different ballpark. After all, the cry we so often hear from the sceptic is, 'Where's the proof?' So, when we ask for and receive 'proof', we can't simply turn round and lightly dismiss it as coincidence. Yet some people explain such things away as 'coincidence' or 'life's unexplained happenings'. But when we actually think about it, isn't this the bottom line – to reach the place where we accept the reality of God and His supernatural abilities without ever being able to understand everything? We either have faith in Him and His overruling ability to perform wonder-working miracles, or we dismiss the evidence as coincidence and in so doing put our lives further and further away from the influence and person of Jesus Christ. So, I suggest there's either a will to believe or a will not to believe. The outworking of the choice we make will either draw us closer to God, or drive us further away from Him.

CHAPTER 9

THE CHRISTIAN IN THE MARKET-PLACE

. . . somewhere in the middle of what God is doing,
when we are unsure of what's happening,
and no matter what our senses are screaming,
we have to rely on the Lord to work things out
His way. That's where faith is tried and tested and
our relationship with God moves onto a new
and deeper level.

My conversion to Christianity had awakened my social conscience but I had much to learn. Around this time I was made aware of the problem faced by ex-prisoners who, due to their lack of education in the past and their potential for problems, were unable to secure regular work. I decided to employ and train a number of men who had made professions of faith in Jesus Christ and were now trying to live as Christians. This, of course, was not easy. First, the trade unions operating their 'closed shop' policy bitterly objected. But I knew my motives were pure and the Lord would overcome any resistance. My senior managers informed me that they had been warned by the shop stewards that if these men attempted to work on the following Monday morning there would be serious industrial repercussions. I suggested that they relaxed and let God take care of it. On the Monday morning when the men arrived to start work there had been an accident in our loading bay involving our forklift truck and a delivery van and a loud argument was underway. By the time the commotion died down the new men were quietly working away. Nothing was said, and there was no trouble! Once again God had placed His hand of peace on the situation.

However, the men themselves had a problem with regular employment and I was to learn how difficult it was for them to adjust to a normal life-style. For example, during their years of unemployment, their electricity bills had been paid by Social Services. This meant they had no financial incentive to turn the heating down and left it operating at full power for most of the time. As they were now in employment, the financial assistance stopped and a major financial problem arose when the electricity bill arrived. I realized that these families had never been taught to budget household expenses, and regular employment after many years of being totally dependent upon Social Services was causing serious problems for them. In such circumstances we found we could help most effectively on an individual and personal basis.

Another challenge we faced was to make sure that we treated Christian workers no differently from non-Christian workers.

I employed a likeable, unemployed young married man professing to be a Christian, but who was soon causing concern because of unexplained absenteeism and bad time-keeping. He always had a convincing excuse, but eyebrows were being raised and eventually he received the statuary 'warning letter'. I then discovered he was drinking alcohol while at work, so a further warning letter was sent. This was followed by a visit to his home to talk with him and his young wife, who was very understanding of my problem with her husband.

I raised this matter with my church elders who had been praying for this young man, and asked them why it was that the more we prayed for this man the worse he became. Their answer was, 'God is probably answering your prayer His way.'

It was a mark of my Christian immaturity that I found this answer difficult to understand. But, hey, there was loads I didn't understand. However, because I was very conscious of having so much to learn about the way God worked, at the time when I became a Christian I had resolved to listen carefully to the wisdom available to me from men and women who had insight into the things of God, acquired through many years of experience. So, I took my elders' advice and continued to act honourably and make sure that my decisions were in accordance with the Bible's teaching.

Shortly afterwards the young man did not appear at work for two days and phoned to say his mother and father had been involved in a terrible car crash and were in hospital with serious injuries. Providentially, I was suspicious and asked what hospital they were in so that I could send some flowers. He told me, but when I contacted the hospital I was informed that they did not have any patients with that name. It transpired that the young man had been on a drinking binge and, unable to get to work, had dreamed up what he thought was an acceptable excuse. I had no option but to terminate his employment despite him pleading with me not to do so. I found this quite distressing but knew that I could not treat this man any differently from the rest of the workforce, Professing a Christian faith or not. I was learning that as a Christian I was expected to do the 'right thing', and in so doing I could allow God to take care of the outcome.

There's a wonderful postscript to this event. A year or so later I was making my way to my parked car when I heard my name being called. I turned to see the young man I had fired. He looked clean and fit and as he bounded across the street towards me the thought crossed my mind that he was going to hit me (it was Glasgow after all!). But no, he shook my hand and said how much he wanted to thank me. I was stunned and asked him what for. He told me that when I fired him he was so shaken that he came to his senses and began to sort out his life and marriage. He finished by saying, 'You were right to fire me. It was a lesson I needed to learn, thank you!' Into my mind came the wise answer from the elders over a year ago and I realized God had answered my prayer His way.

Of course it's a lot easier to say than to do

Let me give you an example of what I mean.

Due to the ongoing pressures of cash flow and the major source of our business coming from my personal contacts, it was necessary to make an effort to reduce overheads by releasing one of my senior colleagues. My other directors confirmed my opinion, but I could not steel myself to make such a painful decision. The man concerned was a good friend and had stood by me through difficult times when the company was growing. I agonised over this personal problem and spent serious time in prayer asking the Lord to make His will clearly known to me.

Some days later, still putting off the decision, I was walking out of our local Christian bookshop and literally bumped into a businessman who was also in the printing trade and whom I knew to be a Christian. We didn't know each other very well and his reaction when he saw me was astonishing. He looked very surprised and said to me, 'I have a message from God for you.' Appearing as surprised as I was he continued, 'I've to tell you 1st Chronicles 28:20 from the Authorised Version. I don't know what it means for you, but God clearly told me to pass it on to you when we met!'

Nothing remotely like this had ever happened to me before (nor to him) and I wasn't too sure how to react. I acknowledged what he had to say, thanked him, went to my car and opened my Authorised Version (KJV) of the Bible. Turning to the appropriate passage I read:

'Be strong and of good courage, and do it: fear not, nor be dismayed: for the LORD God, even my God, will be with thee; he will not fail thee, nor forsake thee, until thou hast finished all the work for the service of the house of the LORD.'

I sat transfixed with God's word, '*Do it*' hammering into my brain. I took it to be the answer I was waiting for and God's confirmation to go ahead and ask my colleague to leave the company.

At the time none of us knew what was about to happen to the company and it seemed hard on my colleague. However, in the end he actually benefited financially. The lesson for me was that God knows the future and allows situations to develop where the only correct way is God's way. When we hear His voice, but most importantly, confirmed in His Word, we must trust and obey in the knowledge that there's no other and no better way.

Understandably, this incident made a deep impression on me and I came to the conclusion that God was, in fact, doing something wonderful that would radically affect my life and I was in the middle of a miracle. My thinking was that at some stage in the recorded biblical miracles, those involved would have wondered what was happening, while at the same time being aware that something supernatural was unfolding. For example, Jesus instructing the servants to fill the huge stone water jars with water when the wine ran out; or when He told His disciples to make the people sit down and as He prayed over five small loaves and two fishes; or when He commanded that the stone be rolled away from Lazarus' tomb. With hindsight, we can see how the miracles worked out and it's marvellous. But somewhere in the process of what God is doing, when we are unsure of what's happening, and no matter what our senses are screaming, we have to be prepared to pour the water into the jars, tell the people to be seated and wait on Jesus, and roll that stone out of the way. We have to rely on the Lord to work things out His way.

That's where faith is tried and tested and our knowledge of God and our personal relationship with Jesus moves onto a new and deeper level.

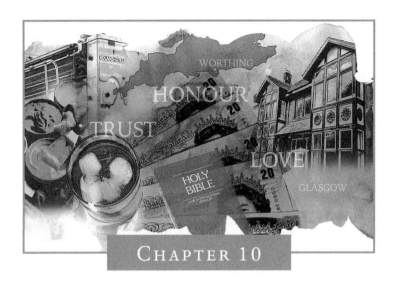

CHAPTER 10

THE BEGINNING
OF
THE END

*. . . while I was often perplexed and hard pressed,
and all that goes with it, it was exciting, stimulating
and utterly wonderful to go through what was a
unique time in my life, and as I found my faith
tried, tested and strengthened I personally learned
a great deal about my Father God from the
experience . . . [the dilemma] is the awful feeling
that comes from being despised and an object of
gossip and scorn, but knowing all the time
that God's hand is at work and that things
are not what they appear to be.*

To add to our financial difficulties, the bitter recession of the early eighties was taking its toll and two of our largest customers in the confectionery/food industry, failed to solve their own financial crises and went into receivership, causing us major problems. The difficulty was compounded by the fact that we had recently agreed to sell some existing printing machines and purchase a new web-press to open up a new paperback production line. The binding machinery was already installed and running and further negotiations were in hand regarding the printing press.

Suddenly, the future looked bleak and I could see no way out of this crisis. My diary from March 1985 records me confessing to a feeling that a 'humbling process is underway and probably there's a lot more humbling in the near future'.

Then something most unusual happened that I've never been able to get to the bottom of. I was informed that a company with a name very similar to our own had closed down and, as word spread, misinformed gossip mixed with the truth that we had cash flow problems caused suppliers to panic and begin legal moves to secure payment. Within forty-eight hours our financial situation became untenable, and I was advised to call in the official receiver and cease trading.

I will never forget sitting at my office desk debating with myself whether to call in the receiver. Should I close the company and face the personal nightmare that would follow, or should I once again attempt a financial rescue operation of the type I had successfully achieved several times in the past year or so? As I deliberated, my office door opened and the production manager gave me some further bad news: a gear had stripped in one of our large printing presses and it had ground to a halt.

I had the overwhelming sense of the Lord letting me know that the company was to close and I could either do it His way and make the phone call to the receiver, or He would disable every machine in the factory and there would be nothing left. I made the phone call and the company passed into the hands of the official receiver. So began an incredibly painful, yet spiritually rewarding experience through which I learned that the end could be the beginning.

When David was going through a particularly trying time before he became king of Israel, he wrote Psalm 109, which has been entitled the 'Song of the Slandered'. The psalm describes the reactions of a man who has been unjustly accused and wrongly treated by those who were attempting to destroy him without reasonable cause. In verses 25–27 he cries:

'I am an object of scorn to my accusers;
    when they see me, they shake their heads.
Help me, O LORD my God;
    save me in accordance with your love.
Let them know that it is your hand,
    that you, O LORD, have done it.'

David is asking God to vindicate him, but to do it in such a way as to reveal the fact that it is God who is doing it. Do you see the dilemma? It is the awful feeling that comes from being despised, and an object of gossip and scorn, but knowing all the time that God's hand is at work and that things are not what they appear to be to the average on-looker. The Old Testament prophets certainly suffered this way, but surely the obvious example was the cross. Wasn't Jesus despised and rejected? Didn't the onlookers sneer and scorn? Yet all the while God was working out His salvation plan for the human race through the pain and suffering of His Son, and though it was Friday, Sunday was coming!

As Christians, when we go through times when we are misunderstood and our motives are called into question – although, frustratingly, we know that we are rightly and properly held to be accountable and responsible as far as the world around us is concerned – we are aware that things are not what they seem, because God is doing something by allowing unpleasant things to happen to us to advance His plan and purpose in our lives. Then we, too, must hold on to the fact that it may be like 'Friday ... but Sunday's coming'! The biblical example is Job, who lost his family and possessions and was accused of being a sinful man and getting what he deserved. But, the reader knows that Job was suffering precisely because he was a righteous man and God was using him as a shining example to Satan and us. And Job was rewarded handsomely at the end of his experience. The lesson for us is not to expect a trouble-free life as a Christian, but to remember the examples set before us in Scripture. In times like this prayer is the only course of action, and, believe me, I did not need any encouragement to pray. God's promises are also a source of great comfort; for example:

> 'From everyone who has been given much, much will be demanded; and from the one who has been entrusted with much, much more will be asked.'   (Luke 12:48)

To some, that promise may seem threatening, while others may find it incomprehensible, but I knew I had been given much. I had been dramatically brought into the Christian faith through a 'Damascus Road' experience. I had been delivered from alcohol addiction. I had been given back my wife and family and had personally experienced God working in quite breathtaking ways. Common sense, together with all I had learned about the ways of God, told me that this new heart-breaking experience was for a purpose. And while *'much will be demanded'* may sound ominous, I knew that God was no hard task-master: He was my heavenly Father who had good plans and purposes for my life, as He says in Jeremiah 29:11:

> *' "For I know the plans I have for you," declares the* Lord, *"plans to prosper you and not to harm you, plans to give you hope and a future." '*

Then, remembering the example of the Israelites in Exodus 14:10–14, who panicked when they saw the Egyptian army coming after them but were told by Moses that the Lord would fight for them and they only had to stay still, I knew that I had to get on with my everyday life and do whatever had to be done, allowing God to show His power and love for those who have an eye to see and an ear to hear. He did! This is how . . .

In order to raise the finances to pay our outstanding debt, the receiver sensibly wanted to finish the manufacture of the many thousands of part-completed books that were still on the production line. This meant that no new orders would be accepted and all work in progress would be completed, invoiced and dispatched to the customers. With no new orders coming in, we would not require our full workforce and could let people go as each department completed its work and closed.

We had several types of printing presses and most of our printers were trained to operate one specific type. Only two men could operate all the machines. To complete the remaining orders on all the printing machines we needed these two operators to stay with us during this time. With the exception of these two men, all our printers found new positions in other companies within twenty-four hours and handed in their notice. The two 'all-rounders' remained with us and over the next few weeks completed the outstanding printing! Only then did they receive new positions.

Our photo-litho/plate-making department was staffed by eight people. Again, we only needed one all-rounder to supply the printing plates for the presses and handle the many tasks in the run-down period ahead. We only had one man capable of carrying out this task. Believe it or not, within the week the other seven had left for new employment and the all-rounder did not find a new position until his work with us was completed.

Despite my feelings of loss, confusion and shame, this quite extraordinary series of coincidences dared me to believe that I was detecting the hand of God controlling the events. It was a glimmer of light in a very dark place, for my greatest fear was that I was out of God's will. Then the flickering light became a lighthouse.

The final and vital stage of book production was the bindery. There, machinery mechanically gathered the printed pages, glued and wrapped the book cover around them and then trimmed the book to size. In order to pay our creditors it was essential that the tons of printed pages were successfully made into books on our new binding line. Everything depended on our bindery manager who was the only person trained to supervise the working of the new machinery and so keep production flowing. But there was a problem: he, with some other colleagues, had decided to use their experience and contacts to open their own printing company at a location some distance away. I fully appreciated their position. They had families and mortgages and there was no way I could, or would, want to get in the way of their future plans. But the loss of our bindery manager when we were about to finish thousands upon thousands of books really concerned me. However, God intervened. Out of the blue, the manager got a phone call from the local council saying that they had heard he was planning to open a new company and they offered him an empty factory across the road from our premises. They said he could have it for a 'peppercorn' rent for a year, after which they would negotiate a future commercial rent. The offer was accepted and from then on, when our binding line jammed, we only had to call across the road and our ex-bindery manager would pop over and fix the problem. Disaster was averted and I had the glorious assurance that God was actively in control of all the events. I still did not know why He had allowed it all to happen, and still asked Him why, but those 'God-incidents' proved to me that God was most definitely in control, and that, more than anything, was what I needed to know as the consequences began to hurt.

We had remortgaged our house to help fund the business expansion and now as the debt mounted we found we were going to lose our family home. Loans I had confidently signed for as guarantor in past years suddenly and unexpectedly had to be repaid. And to make matters infinitely worse the Inland Revenue informed me that my income tax, which had been handled by our accountants, had been underpaid and I owed them a substantial sum. This meant that the rebate we were depending upon was going to be reduced to a pitiful amount.

Repeatedly, I went before the Lord in tears and asked Him, 'Why? Why was this happening?' I reminded Him of our devotion and faithfulness, of all the good things our company had achieved for so many people. It just seemed so unfair. Yet, though battered and bruised, my basic faith was never in doubt. I knew better than to measure God's love by the success or failure of a printing company. Sure, I did not know why, and yes, it was appalling, but my wife was like a rock and our children, though bewildered by the events unfolding around them and the sweeping downward changes to their life-style, coped magnificently.

I remember some businessmen arriving at our factory to examine the possibility of buying the company as a going concern. While they were being shown around one of them winked in a conspiratorial manner and said, 'You got everything in the wife's name, eh? Got the BMW tucked away round the corner?' In reply, I said, 'I'm Christian and everything is open and above-board. There's nothing tucked away – if I lose it, I lose it.' I will never forget the look of contempt on his face. But if this life is all you have to look forward to, then it is not surprising you would do anything to make it that little bit better. If, however, you believe the promise from the lips of Jesus that this life is the pathway to glory and your future is determined by your present decisions, then, no matter what the difficulties and problems, you view everything differently. Paul summed it up perfectly in 2 Corinthians 4:18, where after recounting the trials and difficulties of this life, he said:

'We fix our eyes not on what is seen, but on what is unseen. For what is seen is temporary, but what is unseen is eternal.'

I received a phone call from the *Daily Record*, Scotland's largest selling newspaper. The reporter asked me, 'How could this happen to you?' I replied, 'What do you mean?'

He said, 'You recognise Jesus as Chairman of your company, you start with a prayer meeting on Monday mornings and have a Bible study on Thursdays. You don't print offensive literature or supply the drinks industry, so tell me why should this happen to you?' I realized someone had phoned the newspaper with our story and I was concerned for the Christian witness and name of Jesus.

Here I was to learn another valuable lesson. There is a promise from Scripture in Matthew 10:19–20 and repeated in Luke 12:11–12, that when under pressure for the kingdom's sake we are not to worry about what we are to say for the words will be given to us by our Father in heaven.

I found myself saying to the reporter, 'You misunderstand the Christian message. If we were promised that by becoming a Christian, we would have a secure job and a healthy bank account, the churches would be filled to capacity and people would be queuing outside to join. The truth is, Jesus said, "Take up your cross," not, "Pick up your flexible friend."' I continued, 'Christians are not promised a smooth journey, but are promised a safe arrival.' He politely thanked me and fortunately nothing harmful was printed.

I was so sure that God was controlling events that I was able to make a prophecy.

Two months had passed and it was my last Friday. All the books had been dispatched and invoiced. The factory was cleaned and ready for the auction of machinery and material on the following Monday, though I would not be there to witness it. Working with me was a Christian, a young married man who had been unable to find new employment despite a number of interviews over the previous months. He was the last of the workforce and along with me he, too, would be finishing that Friday. During the morning I said to him, 'I really don't know what God is doing, but I know He has needed you here with me and now your work is completed you will find a new position.' Later that morning he received a telephone call from a company with whom he had already had an interview telling him the job was his and could he start on Monday. Praise God!

I drove home for the last time. The future seemed bleak – yet I had the assurance that God was with me. And though my emotions were in turmoil I remembered His word to me from Jeremiah 29:11: *'I know the plans I have for you . . . plans to prosper you and not to harm you, plans to give you a hope and a future.'* I just had to hold on in there and allow God to work out His plan and purpose for my life especially when going through painful and unfamiliar circumstances; for example, 'signing on' as unemployed.

Distasteful and humiliating for someone who had prided himself on being in control of his life this was something that had to be done. Our finances were in meltdown and everything we had worked so hard for – our home and business – was being taken from us. Sitting outside the employment office in an old, rusty motor car that had been kindly loaned to us by a Christian friend, was very different from sitting in the up-market executive car I was used to. With a mounting sense of apprehension I watched crowds of unemployed people entering the Social Services' office, and out of the blue a clear voice within me taunted, 'Christianity has brought you to this!' I did not mistake it or imagine it; it was as clear as a bell within my head, 'Christianity has brought you to this!'

All the emotions of pain, loss, hurt, bewilderment assaulted me and in tears I cried out, 'Oh Jesus! Help me!' Immediately, I sensed the peaceful but all-powerful presence of the Lord. He said to me, 'Look at all the people.

They are lost, but you have Me, and your position is far from what it seems.' This sort of experience is not easy to explain but immediately with a renewed resolve I entered the building and 'signed on' as unemployed. I then found myself offering help to someone who could not read a form, giving directions to a man who could not read English, and smiling politely to men and women who were unsure and anxious in what so easily could appear to be an unsympathetic environment. Truly, things are not what they seem.

I received a wonderful confirmation of this truth the following Saturday. Some months previously, I had been invited to speak about my Christian faith at an evangelistic event in Kilmarnock. The man who spoke that evening was not the successful businessman originally invited. Instead, he was an unemployed man who told the story of God's faithfulness and love through his recent business failure. At the end of the evening, responding to the evangelist's invitation, a number of people came forward to make professions of faith in Jesus Christ and, wonder of wonders, every one of them was unemployed. I realized that the unemployed man who spoke to them about the love and faithfulness of God through life's real difficulties had much more in common with them than the successful business-man originally invited to speak. Later that night I drove home to Glasgow in that rusty old motor car rejoicing in my heart and singing God's praises. My Father in heaven knew what He was doing. My place was to trust Him to work out my future. God had touched me, and my desires, dreams, hopes and aspirations were now all changed. I simply wanted to serve Him and tell others of His wonderful love. My future was in His hands. But what of the consequences for others?

Obviously, it was not my intention to lose my business and our home; on the contrary, it was my great desire to build a strong and prosperous family business. While I deeply regretted any loss suffered by others, I lost far more than anyone else, so it was not the case that I prospered while others paid the price.

The fact that it was two of my customers going into receivership that caused our financial position to become untenable is a reminder that there are no guarantees that any business will be immune from loss. I found some consolation in that we were a limited liability company, a precaution taken precisely to limit shareholders' and directors' personal liability in the event of financial loss. As a Christian businessman I had to act honourably and obey God's law and the law of the land. Hence, as I have already explained, there were no shady dealings; everything was done 'above-board'. As far as I was aware, every one of my former employees found gainful employment and that gave me great peace of mind.

When the not easily answered question, 'Why does God allow things like this to happen?' raised its head, I took comfort in my belief that, as the whole event was under God's control, He would have His plan and purpose even in the strange and paradoxical circumstances everyone involved went through. Although we would like to have them, there are often no straightforward answers to this type of question. God tells us that His ways are not our ways, and for the Christian this means that we simply have to trust that God knows what He is doing and believe the promise of Romans 8:28:

'...in all things God works for the good of those who love him, who have been called according to his purpose.'

I found the following legend helpful . . .

Moses once sat meditating near a well. A traveller stopped to drink from the well and, when he did so, his purse fell from his waist into the sand. The man went on his way and soon afterwards a second man passed near the well, saw the purse, picked it up and continued on his journey. Some time later a third man stopped at the well to relieve his thirst and, sitting down, fell asleep in the hot sun. Meanwhile, the first man had discovered his purse was missing and, assuming he must have lost it at the well, returned and awoke the third man (who of course knew nothing) and demanded his money back. An argument ensued and the enraged first man killed the third man.

Moses then said to God, 'You see why men do not believe in You? There is too much evil and injustice in the world. Why should the first man have lost his purse and become a murderer? Why should the second get a purse full of gold without having worked for it? The third was completely innocent. Why was he killed?

God answered, 'For once, and only once, I will give you an explanation. I cannot do this every time. The first man was a thief's son. The purse contained money stolen by his father from the father of the second man who, finding the purse, only found what was due to him. The third was a murderer whose crime had never been detected and who received from the first the punishment he deserved. In the future believe there is sense and righteousness in what transpires even when you do not understand.'

That certainly gives much food for thought. However, another question asked of my circumstances is: 'Does all that happened to you mean that God's work doesn't last, and that all you did for Him was a waste of time?' This is the implicit criticism behind the taunt, 'Christianity has brought you to this!' I was now unemployed and had lost everything that I had worked so hard to achieve. So why did God cause a series of thrilling miraculous events to happen in such a wonderful way, if a year or two later everything was to come to nothing? It's a fair question.

When I thought about this, I realized that it is my selfish fallen nature that wants life to work out to my plan. After Jesus raised people from the dead, in the course of natural events they later all died. The day after miraculously feeding the 5,000, the same men, women and children were hungry and had to find their own food. In other words, we are wrong to presume that God's miraculous intervention in our lives necessarily removes ongoing causes and effects or nullifies natural laws for ever after. The supernatural can, and does, move in and out of our lives' circumstances weaving its own plan and purpose. And, although this carries the danger of accusing God of being capricious, like the Greek and Roman gods, and subjecting the human race to His whims, the bottom line is that with the hindsight of twenty years, there is no way that anyone can say, 'It all came to nothing!'

Certainly, the questions can be asked: 'Why did it not all work out as you had expected it to, with the establishment of a long-term successful printing/publishing company? Surely that would have pleased God and saved you and Joyce all the pain and heartache, wouldn't it?' My answer is that my prayer, in harmony with Joyce's, throughout my Christian life had been that God would use me in whatever capacity He saw fit to further His kingdom and bring glory to His name. And while I understandably thought that would be achieved by running a successful printing company producing Christian literature, the Bible makes it very clear that God does not work to our agenda. He has other ideas, and in my case, was using that distressing, yet strangely reassuring experience as a learning curve and training time in preparation for something better; something I could not in my wildest imagination have believed possible. And not only for me or Joyce. Think of this: the events I have described touched the lives of many people, and the manner and way they responded, the lessons they learned or did not learn, the acceptance or rejection of God's hand in their lives, were all part of His grand and glorious plan to advance His kingdom in the hearts of the many men and women affected by our experience. From my perspective, I understood what the apostle Paul meant when he wrote:

'We are hard pressed on every side, but not crushed; perplexed, but not in despair; persecuted, but not abandoned; struck down, but not destroyed.'   (2 Corinthians 4:8–9)

Suffice it to say, while I was often perplexed and hard pressed, and all that goes with it, it was exciting, stimulating and utterly wonderful to go through what was a unique time in my life, and as I found my faith tried, tested and strengthened I personally learned a great deal about my Father God from the experience.

Joyce...

Losing the company was a humbling experience in many ways, but we were always aware of God's presence and control. All the material things we had held so dearly had to go and with them much of our pride. It was the teaching of John 3:30: *'He must become greater; I must become less.'* I continue to be amazed at God's patience and long suffering as He deals with our pride, selfishness, greed and self-righteous attitudes. Having been saved in our older years Satan had had a long time to convince us what hard-working independent good folk we were!

All these wrong attitudes were, and still are, being dealt with so we may one day be changed into His likeness. It seems an impossible task, yet God has promised and I believe Him, for Philippians 1:6 says, *'he who began a good work in you will carry it on to completion.'* And Jude 24 promises: *'[God] is able to keep you from falling and to present you before his glorious presence without fault and with great joy.'* I clung to these promises.

Our company in Scotland eventually closed and we were brought to Worthing to work for CPO. It was hard leaving our family and friends and especially our church family. It was also a great upheaval for our children. Our oldest daughter remained in Glasgow to continue at university and that was difficult for us all. It took a lot of adjusting for the two younger ones; new schools, friends, church etc. It's a different culture in the south, not just a different accent, so there was teasing and other heartaches for them to deal with, much of which even I am unaware.

CHAPTER 11

To the Ends of the Earth – Well, Worthing

*Often I was in unfamiliar, difficult and
even potentially precarious situations –
definitely out of my comfort zone – yet time
and time again God graciously assured me of His
presence and support. As someone who
had made his way through life relying on his
own strength and ability, it was hugely comforting
to discover that the God of all the universe
had His eye on me and that because
He never slumbers or sleeps I could
trust Him completely.*

Some time previously, hoping for fellowship with like-minded business men and women I had allied our company with an 'association of Christian printers'. The largest of these companies was the Christian Publicity Organisation (CPO) based in Worthing, West Sussex. They specialised in printing for evangelical churches with a particular interest in promoting evangelism. I spoke with their general secretary and we arranged to meet and discuss their future plans for marketing and manufacturing and whether I would be able to assist them. At this time I was pursuing a number of possible employment options but I willingly travelled down to Worthing to meet and discuss matters of mutual interest. It became increasingly clear that this was where the Lord wanted me to be and I spent one year working for CPO based in Scotland, travelling throughout the UK fact-finding and preparing a marketing plan for the future. At the same time, drawing upon my printing factory moving experience, I helped to locate larger premises and then relocate their manufacturing plant and offices into a new factory in Worthing. When the relocation to the new premises was completed, it was suggested that I work from Worthing. This of course meant moving from Glasgow, and while Joyce and I were agreeable to the proposal we wanted a definite sign from the Lord that this was His will and purpose for us before we uprooted the family and took them to the other end of the country. So, once again, it was to be a 'fleece' laid before the Lord, and this time I asked Him for two clear signs that moving to CPO in Worthing was His plan for my life and would be right for my family.

The 'fleece' comprised two requests. The first concerned an outstanding debt to American Express. Most people do not realize that sums of money incurred by legitimate business expenses on a company credit card become a personal liability if the company goes into receivership. American Express now insisted that I pay a sum in excess of £1,400, which, of course, after everything else, I did not have. As part of the 'fleece' I rationalised that if we left Scotland the Lord would want our finances to be settled and tidied behind us, so could He please provide a way to pay the amount outstanding to American Express by the end of the month. The second request was that both Joyce and I wanted our Christian colleagues in CPO to confirm that they believed it was God's plan and purpose for the company that we joined them at Worthing. So, the second part of the fleece was that we would receive official confirmation of the offer from CPO by the end of the month.

Towards the end of the month I received a lawyer's letter from American Express demanding payment of £1,442.45 (the original amount plus interest) by return or legal procedings would begin to recover the debt. In the post the following day I received a letter from the Inland Revenue enclosing an income tax rebate for £1,442.72. The cost of the postage stamp to send the cheque and papers to American Express was covered by the 27p difference. I was so impressed by the sheer wonder of this miracle that I photocopied the two letters and still have them as verification. Then the very next day I received a letter from CPO telling me that during a recent day of prayer the entire workforce had fasted and prayed and believed it was the Lord's will that I move to Worthing. The 'fleece' had been answered and we immediately began planning our move to the south coast of England. Praise God!

So followed three wonderful years with CPO during which I had the privilege of establishing a marketing strategy for a

Christian organisation with a ministry close to my heart:
that of equipping the evangelical Church for evangelism.
I travelled the length and breadth of the United Kingdom,
attending Christian conferences, meeting Church leaders
and individual Christian men and women concerned to
reach our generation with the Good News of Jesus.

However, it is not possible to go through circumstances
such as those I had recently experienced without collecting
some 'baggage' and I needed time to come to terms with my
new situation. It was a humbling experience to go from
being the managing director of my own business to being a
member of a fellowship where each member had the same
status and an equal say in the conduct of the business.
However, it was all clarified for me at Worthing Tabernacle,
when listening to Pastor Tony Sargent's series of messages
on the life of Joseph in the Book of Genesis he quoted the
following poem by an unknown author:

> When God wants to drill a man and thrill a man and
>   skill a man,
> When God wants to mould a man to play the noblest
>   part,
> When He yearns with all His heart to create so great
>   and bold a man . . .
> That all the world shall be amazed,
> Watch His methods, watch His ways;
> How He ruthlessly perfects whom He royally elects:
> How He hammers him and hurts him
> And with mighty blows converts him into trial shapes
>   of clay
> Which only God can understand;
> While man's tortured heart is crying and he lifts
>   beseeching hands,

Yet God bends but never breaks when man's good
    He undertakes,
How He uses whom He chooses,
And with mighty power infuses him,
With every act induces him to try His splendour out,
God knows what He's about!

I realized that I was being remade, and in a wonderful way God ministered to me through both my Christian colleagues at CPO and new friends in Worthing Tabernacle as He continued the work of remaking me into the person He wanted me to become. So, while I wholeheartedly gave from my years of print and marketing experience to the work of CPO, I received in return a rebuilding of self-esteem and a much wider knowledge and valuable insight of the Christian Church in the United Kingdom today. Most importantly, God confirmed to me that my life was out-working according to His plan as He continued to bless me with the personal 'God-incidents' that warmed my heart and assured me of His continual presence. The significance of this became apparent when I was travelling around the United Kingdom. Let me give you an example.

One of my marketing strategies was to take the CPO product range on display to town centre Christian book-shops. I had previously written to a thousand or so local customers advising them of my visit and inviting them to come and meet me to obtain new samples and answers to questions regarding the use of the products to meet the needs of their churches.

On this occasion, my display stand was set up in a Christian bookshop in Belfast city centre and because Belfast was in the midst of 'the troubles' I was staying in bed and breakfast accommodation some miles south of the city. My first day had gone well and I enjoyed meeting many CPO customers. The following morning, as I began driving towards the slip-road onto the motorway the exhaust fell off from the silencer box under the car. It was still attached to the car by the rear bracket and with the front end digging into the tarmac I could not drive forwards. It was about 8.30 am and I was due to be at my display stand in the Christian bookshop at 9.15. As it was a twenty-minute drive from this point to the city centre I was in big trouble. I prayed and asked God for help.

Looking beyond the underpass I saw a garage and made for it. By this time it was 8.45. I explained my predicament and the garage staff were terrific, advising me to give them the car keys and the car would be repaired and ready for collection that evening. Terrific, yes, but there I was miles from the city centre at 8.55 with no hope of being at my display stand in the shop by 9.15. Suddenly, I was attracted by a car horn and a driver who had just filled up with petrol waving for me to go over and speak to him. Now this was Northern Ireland at a dangerous time and I hesitated. But, hey, I was desperate and hadn't I just asked the Lord for help? So over I went. The young man introduced himself as a Christian who recognised me from the bookshop the day before and wondered if I needed any help. I explained my predicament and he told me that as his office was 'next door' to the bookshop to hop in and he would give me a lift. I did so and arrived at 9.15. My car was waiting for me at 6.30 pm ready for my journey to Dublin the following morning.

I cannot adequately express how grateful I was to God for these 'happenings'. Often I was in unfamiliar, difficult and even potentially precarious situations – definitely out of my comfort zone – yet time and time again God graciously assured me of His presence and support. As someone who had made his way through life relying on his own strength and ability, it was hugely comforting to discover that the God of all the universe had His eye on me and that because He never slumbers or sleeps I could trust Him completely.

A Chief Executive Remembers
John Milne BA; CEO (retired),
Christian Publicity Organisation, Worthing

*It has been a blessing to see how God has guided
and provided for Hugh and his family over the
intervening years and how He is continuing to bless
Hugh's powerful testimony to God's saving grace.
I am grateful for his brief but valuable time
of service with the ministry of CPO.*

It was in a newspaper article that I first came across Hugh Hill's remarkable testimony to God's saving grace. I was CEO of CPO based in Worthing, West Sussex, and his pressures and problems as the managing director of a large printing company in Scotland struck a cord with me. I thought it would be good to contact him and tell him about the Christian Printing Fellowship, of which we were members, and express the hope that we would have the opportunity to meet up sometime.

I next heard from Hugh when he explained that it had become impossible for him to resolve the intense financial problems of his printing firm and, being forced to close, he was now seeking the Lord's will for his future employment. Hugh had a desire to promote the Christian faith, and as CPO's ministry was to supply the evangelical church with materials for evangelism he travelled down to Worthing and we discussed the possibility of appointing him as CPO sales representative for Scotland. It was a position CPO management had not previously considered but with his marketing background, knowledge of the printing industry, wealth of sales experience and numerous print contacts, we thought we should discuss this possibility more fully.

I subsequently visited Hugh in Glasgow and met a number of potential customers. The outcome was that Hugh was appointed as our Scottish Representative in October 1984. However, within a year of his appointment, it was felt that his scope in Scotland was too limited and he was invited to join the team in Worthing as CPO Sales Director. It meant a big upheaval for him as well as for Joyce and the family but eventually they relocated to Worthing and the Scottish office was closed.

For some time CPO had been looking for new premises to expand their printing and publishing business. The original offices had been developed with three extensions providing 6,000 sq. ft of floor space but more was still needed. Eventually suitable premises were located with 16,000 sq. ft of floor space and the complicated move was made in March 1986. Hugh was able to play a major role in determining the best way to allocate and layout the available space. An additional benefit in having larger premises meant that we could invite the media deptartment of Arab World Ministries to join us in the new complex and also provide office space for

Bientôt, a gospel broadsheet ministry. Later, the UK office of Middle East Media was relocated at CPO.

Hugh's role as Sales Director involved him in a great deal of travelling throughout the United Kingdom representing CPO at numerous Christian conferences, Bible colleges and meetings with individuals and church groups concerned with local evangelism. However, by 1988 Hugh was sure the Lord was calling him to leave the printing industry and undertake theological training with a view to ordination into the preaching/teaching ministry. Hugh responded to God's call and resigned from CPO in June 1988.

It has been a blessing to see how God has guided and provided for Hugh and his family over the intervening years and is continuing to bless Hugh's powerful testimony to God's saving grace. I am grateful for his brief but valuable time of service with the ministry of CPO.

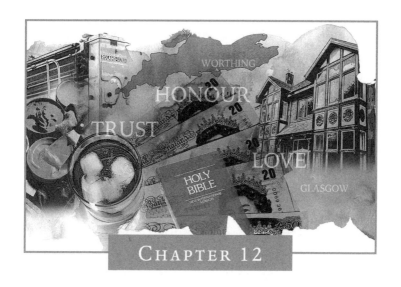

CHAPTER 12

GOD'S CALL
TO THE
PREACHING/
TEACHING MINISTRY

Preparing to go to full-time Bible college
for two years at forty-eight years of age and
moving into what for me was an unknown
situation far removed from my comfort zone
had the potential to be disastrous, so the
confirmation that this was God's plan and
purpose for my life was a great assurance to me
and Joyce. We knew everything
was going to be all right!

With the benefit of hindsight, the call to full-time ministry should not have come as a surprise. Although it was my heart's desire, as far as I was concerned there was absolutely no way it could happen. After all that Joyce and the family had been through following the loss of our company, we had no savings and I was working for a Christian organisation that paid wages on a 'needs only basis'.

I had been visiting CPO customers in Wales, and late in the evening I was driving home from Cardiff to Worthing. After hearing my testimony and aware of my love of the gospel, the Christians with whom I had been staying told me that they thought I should consider training for the 'ministry', and one lady expressed the strong view that I should go to Bible college. This was all passing through my mind as I drove home and as usual I turned it into a prayer. I told the Lord that I would dearly love to go to Bible college and train for a preaching ministry, but as I could not put Joyce through more uncertainty and possible hardship He would have to 'take care of Joyce'. I do realize how that may sound, but remembering all that Joyce had to contend with since the loss of our company and the life-style that it afforded, to say nothing of our beautiful home, I felt that it was only fair that Joyce should be certain of God's will for our future. Only then would she be able to gladly accept whatever changes God had in mind for our family, secure in the knowledge that to be in God's will was the place of blessing.

When I arrived home Joyce had just returned from the mid-week church Bible study/prayer meeting which had been led by the godly Bible teacher, Leith Samuel. She told me that in the middle of his address Leith stopped and said something to the effect that 'he believed because of their life experience mature men should think of going to Bible college'. Joyce then said to me, 'When he said that I thought of you. Maybe you should think about it!' The coincidence was quite overwhelming, and after telling Joyce about my recent experience with the folk in Cardiff and my prayer during the homeward journey, we agreed that I should take positive action in seeking God's direction for training for the 'full-time ministry'.

Then, of course, came the doubts and fears: 'Who am I to think of a preaching/teaching ministry?' But hey, isn't Saul [Paul] the perfect example of the man you would least expect to end up at Bible college? You can read his pre-Christian CV in Philippians 3:5–6:

> 'Circumcised on the eighth day, of the people of Israel, of the tribe of Benjamin, a Hebrew of Hebrews; in regard to the law, a Pharisee; as for zeal, persecuting the church; as for legalistic righteousness, faultless.'

This religious zealot was hauling Christians out of their homes and murdering them when he was called by Jesus and in Acts 9:5 we find him lying blinded in the dust of the Damascus Road asking, *'Who are you, Lord?'* Jesus replied, *'I am Jesus, whom you are persecuting . . . Now get up and go into the city, and you will be told what you must do'* (Acts 9:5–6). So began the life-changing process that transformed Saul of Tarsus into the apostle Paul.

This greatly encouraged me and should encourage others; we are in glorious company. Moses, Joshua, Gideon, Jeremiah – all giants of the faith and men mightily used by God who when first called by Him were afraid because they knew they were not up to it. Moses pleaded, *'O Lord, please send someone else to do it'* (Exodus 4:13). Joshua was so obviously uptight that the Lord repeatedly encouraged him with the promise, *'As I was with Moses, so I will be with you;*

I will never leave you nor forsake you' (Joshua 1:5). Listen to Gideon's reply to the Lord's call for him to be the one to save Israel: *'But Lord . . . how can I save Israel? My clan is the weakest in Manasseh, and I am the least in my family'* (Judges 6:15). And how about Jeremiah's excuse: *'Ah, Sovereign* Lord *. . . I do not know how to speak; I am only a child'* (Jeremiah 1:6). For me, the bottom line is I cannot do it, but I know a Man who can, and His name is Jesus: *'I can do everything through him who gives me strength'* (Philippians 4:13).

In the following weeks I contacted various Bible colleges and the call of God for me to attend London Theological Seminary was confirmed by my church leaders in June. Although I had no financial provision, I knew it was important for me to move ahead in faith, so I immediately telephoned the college and reserved a place for the coming October and gave two months' notice to CPO to cease my employment. I then respectfully reminded the Lord of what I had done and asked Him to honour my faith and confirm His call.

I sensed a prompting within me to write to the Inland Revenue explaining my situation and to ask whether I was due any tax rebate. To be honest, considering all that had happened in the recent past I didn't hold out much hope but thought that it would do no harm to follow the 'prompting'. To my utter amazement I received an income tax rebate for the exact amount of my first year's fees at Bible college. Years later, I still shake my head in wonder and awe at the way God works. But what thrilled me more than anything was not the money, although that was wonderful, but the realization that God had my future in His hands and was working it out to His agenda. I now knew with utter certainty that as God wanted me to have training to become a Bible preacher/teacher it would all work out and I need not be overly concerned. This was vitally important. Preparing to go to full-time Bible college for two years at forty-eight years of age and moving into what for me was an unknown situation far removed from my comfort zone had the potential to be disastrous, so the confirmation that this was God's plan and purpose for my life was a great assurance to me and Joyce. We knew everything was going to be all right!

Over the following months, gifts, pledges of support and promises of financial help from friends and church members made it all possible, and I enrolled at London Theological Seminary in October as planned.

Unknown to me, this all coincided with a small evangelical church in Maybridge (a mainly council housing scheme located in West Worthing) having declined in numbers to fourteen elderly members, asking Worthing Tabernacle for help. The outcome was that my church elders decided that I should lead a team of volunteers in an attempt to restore the Maybridge church. I think they figured I couldn't do much harm with fourteen elderly people. Practically, this meant that I travelled up to London on Monday evenings and attended Bible college from Tuesday to Friday. I preached at Maybridge every Sunday and worked full-time for the church during the Easter, summer and Christmas vacations. During these times I engaged in a wide variety of evangelistic activities to introduce the local folk to the church and in the goodness of God the church was indeed restored.

Throughout my two years at Bible college God continued to confirm to me His presence and support through very personal 'God-incidents'. Let me recount one such episode.

Every Monday evening I travelled up to the Bible college in north London ready for the study week which began on

Tuesday morning. On this particular week the staff of London Transport had called a strike and there were no tubes or buses operating on Monday. I set out by train from Worthing to Victoria not knowing how I was to get out to the college at Finchley, but confident that the Lord would help me.

On board the train I could not help but notice an elderly lady who was sharing the carriage. Her arm was in plaster supported by a sling, and as well as lots of luggage she also had a cat in a cage. At Victoria Station I helped her down onto the platform and replying to my offer of further help to find a taxi, she told me that she had ordered a porter to help her and hired a car to meet her. I stifled the 'you'll be lucky' reply and walked away to find some method of transport to Finchley. At the end of the platform I looked back and there was the lady, arm in sling, standing all alone surrounded by her luggage and cat. I couldn't leave her like that, so I walked back and lifting her luggage said, 'I'll help you to your car.'

When she identified the private taxi she had ordered, she asked me, 'Can I give you a lift?'

'Well that depends,' I replied, adding, 'where are you going?'

'I'm going to Finchley,' she said.

'So am I,' I smiled.

'Whereabouts?' she asked.

'Hendon Road.'

'So am I,' she said. Then, 'Whereabouts in Hendon Road?'

'London Theological Seminary,' I answered.

'I live next door to it!' she said.

Well, I ask you! London is forty miles long and twenty miles wide, with a population of well over ten million people and this lady was offering me a lift during a city-wide transport strike to her home which was next door to my destination. I tell you, it felt good.

But it got better. En route, the lady disclosed that she was a clairvoyant and had a healing ministry (which in view of the broken arm I thought was quite amusing: that must have been one she missed) and didn't know anything about Jesus. So, for the rest of the journey I was able to explain the gospel of Jesus to this kind, but needy, lady.

After two wonderful years of Bible teaching and practical learning I was ordained into the Christian ministry at Worthing Tabernacle and I spent a further two exciting and memorable years as pastor of Maybridge Christian Fellowship and rejoiced as the church fellowship grew and blossomed.

A Bible College Principal Remembers
Philip Eveson BA (University of Wales, Bangor),
MA (University of Cambridge, Selwyn College),
MTh (University of London, King's College)

One could not help but be impressed by his pleasant disposition and enthusiasm for the work of the gospel. He was a warm-hearted person, always encouraging other students and helpful to the staff.

Hugh came to the London Theological Seminary (LTS) in October 1988 from Worthing Tabernacle on the south coast of England where Tony Sargent was the minister. At that time Hugh had been given the responsibility of leading a new daughter church, Maybridge Christian Fellowship. LTS specialises in training men for a preaching/pastoral ministry.

It was founded in 1977 by leaders from a wide range of evangelical churches in the United Kingdom under the chairmanship of Dr Martyn Lloyd-Jones.

The curriculum was designed to ensure that it met the needs of those preparing to minister God's Word rather than the requirements of secular examination authorities. For that reason it remains independent of the UK secular academic system. The course is, however, intellectually challenging as well as being spiritually enlivening. The full-time course lasts for two years and covers all the main disciplines associated with theological training. Student progress is evaluated by the method of continuous assessment rather than the examination system. The faculty members are all experienced church leaders which means they offer practical help concerning the day-to-day issues that crop up in the fellowship of the church and in people's lives. Many a discussion started in the lecture room has continued over the dining-room table. The aim of the course is to help men develop effective godly ministries.

Aged forty-seven, Hugh was one of the older students and having only been a Christian for about six years there was much about theology that he did not know. But his commercial background, desire to learn and conviction of God's calling to a preaching ministry, all helped train him for his future career.

For the two years Hugh was with us he preached every Sunday at Maybridge and worked full-time during Christmas, Easter and summer vacations building up the church. One could not help but be impressed by his pleasant disposition and enthusiasm for the work of the gospel. He was a warm-hearted person, always encouraging other students and helpful to the staff. Hugh came to us with all the freshness of a person saved from a non-Christian background and was always excited about the Lord who had rescued him. He was imaginative in his presentations and I well remember, for the first morning devotions that he took at the seminary, he asked my daughter, who was studying art at the time, to draw and cut out a large wine bottle as a visual aid for his sermon during which he put alcohol on trial for its crimes against humanity.

Leaving behind a growing church in Worthing in 1992, Hugh responded to God's call and moved to the Slade Evangelical Church in Plumstead, London, where his ministry was blessed by a large number of men and women being converted, baptised and beginning the Christian life. After eight years Hugh moved to Thomas Cooper Memorial Baptist Church in Lincoln where as pastor for seven years in the goodness of God the Church was blessed by spiritual and numerical growth.

We at LTS are pleased to have played our part in Hugh's training for the full-time ministry and praise God for the way in which He has used him over the years.

CHAPTER 13

FOUR VERY DIFFERENT TESTIMONIES

Over my twenty years in full-time public ministry it has been my privilege and pleasure to be involved in leading many men and women to faith in Jesus Christ, to baptise them in obedience to God's Word and help them grow in their new-found belief (see Matthew 28:19–20). I never cease to be amazed by the transformation brought about in the lives of men and women who find Jesus Christ and make Him Lord of their lives. Where previously there was darkness and discouragement, now there is light and hope. Addictions are broken as men and women are set free from the debilitating effects of drugs and alcohol. Those involved in perverted sex resulting from love growing cold discover a new warmth and passion so that marriages and families are healed and restored. Above all, there is a new sense of purpose for living, a goal to aim for and a new agenda to live by.

What follows is a selection of testimonies from four very different men and women that it has been my privilege to baptise.

A Solicitor's Conveyancer
David F. J. Ginns LLB

My dependency upon alcohol having completely taken over, I was in substantial debt, my marriage was crumbling and I was on a final warning from my firm. It all looked pretty bleak but, thankfully, God was taking a special interest me even though I wasn't aware of it.

Let me take you back to 4.30 pm on Friday, 5th September, 1992. When I woke up that morning little did I know that this would be the day when God would work a miracle in my life and put me into a condition in which I could make a decision that would result in my salvation.

My story, sadly, is unremarkable. I was (and I still am) a conveyancer with a firm of solicitors. This had been my profession ever since I graduated from university in the mid-1970s. I was married to Sue and had two fine sons, but I also had a big problem – only too common in the legal profession I'm afraid – and that was I had been drinking excessively for most of my adult life, but especially for the last ten years or so. By 1992 I was in a bad way. My dependency upon alcohol having completely taken over, I was in substantial debt, my marriage was crumbling and I was on a final warning from my firm. It all looked pretty bleak but, thankfully, God was taking a special interest me even though I wasn't aware of it.

Looking back over their lives, Christians can see quite clearly that God's hand has been on them ever since they can remember. I am no exception and I can see now that a number of events led up to my conversion. My wife had become a Christian four years previously; my brother Simon had converted earlier in 1992; I had been involved in a number of drink-related car crashes but had always somehow emerged with body and driving licence intact. But the event which God used to pull all these strands together was the arrival of Hugh Hill in July 1992 as the new minister at the church where my wife had come to faith; the Slade Evangelical Church in Plumstead, SE London. Sue had ensured that I heard a tape of Hugh's testimony and I learned that his background was similar to mine. Like me, he had been a businessman with a drink problem before God had intervened in his life to remove his craving for alcohol, subsequently leading him to become a Christian and entering the full-time ministry.

The significance of the 5th September, 1992, is that Sue and I were due to go to Hugh's home for dinner. Hugh and his wife Joyce had been working through the list of church members to get to know them better and Sue's turn had now arrived. But my last drink on that Friday afternoon meant that I was

too drunk to go, much to my embarrassment and
much to Sue's angry disappointment. By Saturday
morning, however, I had sobered up and, what's
more, I felt significantly different; that old craving
had suddenly disappeared. That wonderful feeling,
I remember, was such a great release. I contacted
Hugh to apologise for my behaviour and in response
he invited me to the manse to take part in a short
series of basic Bible studies. My brother Simon
came with me, partly to hold my hand and partly
because he was due to be baptised at the Slade on
21st September. And that was when I first believed
with heart and mind; on Sunday, 21st September,
1992, just before Simon entered the water.

What's happened since? I found that the Christian
life, while more demanding in some ways, is
infinitely more interesting than the old life. I have
found myself involved in situations and ministries
which I would not have believed possible sixteen
years ago. I have served as the administrator of my
church for six years, I currently serve as a house-
group leader, I have an occasional preaching ministry
and I am called upon from time to time to provide
legal and spiritual support in all sorts of unusual and
intriguing situations. I have had the intense pleasure
of sharing with Hugh the baptism of both of my
sons, who continue to walk closely with the Lord.
One of them is in his final year at Bible college and
looks to enter full-time ministry later this year. Sue
and I celebrated our silver wedding anniversary last
year, against all the odds, humanly speaking. Our
finances are completely stabilised and earlier this
year we were given an absolutely wonderful gift

from heaven in the form of our first grandchild, who is such a treasure. Had it not been for God's outstandingly gracious intervention in my life, and had it not been for Hugh's willingness to help and support at a such a crucial time, none of these things would have happened. Indeed, I doubt that I would have survived this long.

Perhaps I could conclude by saying this: it so happens that my conversion was a dramatic one, and one which I can pinpoint virtually to the minute, but I am the first to recognise that it is God's sovereign choice to deal with His children in different ways and that there are many who know without doubt that they are Christians but are not able to say exactly when their conversion took place. It's important to remember that whatever our conversion experience may have been, there was no more rejoicing in heaven at my conversion than there was, or will be, for anyone else's. I do hope that this testimony has been an encouragement to those who read it. None of it is my doing, it is all of God and His gracious willingness to save me from myself.

A Sheltered Housing Scheme Manager
Linda C. Brooks – Spiritual Pilgrim

It didn't matter where I went or what I did, something was missing from my life and I became ever more dissatisfied with my lot. Life was becoming quite grim and with family problems and a job that demanded more than I felt able to give I was struggling to cope. My everyday phrase became 'there must be more to life

> *than this'. Anti-depressants didn't help and the*
> *ability to consume ever-larger quantities of alcohol*
> *just left me with a headache.*

I was very rebellious as a child and my father was always telling me to conform. When I left school I joined the Royal Air Force and met my first husband while serving in Cyprus. He was a Jamaican and my parents were quite horrified when we got married. It was definitely not my Dad's idea of conforming! After our son was born I was asked politely not to darken my parents' doorstep again. I went to live in Jamaica but when my marriage broke down I returned to England with my young son.

Sadly, my second husband was an alcoholic and I spent sixteen years in a very unhappy relationship. During this marriage my second son was born. I had both of my sons baptised into the Anglican Church and looking back on that now I think it was for me an attempt to become respectable and accepted by my parents. I was confirmed as an adult and began to attend church, but this did not last long.

My second marriage broke up and I was on my own again. There was something missing in my life and I so wanted to be accepted by my family. My brothers seemed to have done everything right and were highly respected characters. I was to discover later on that Jesus loves me and accepts me just as I am. I don't have to earn His love, and when you know that in your heart nothing else matters. Everything that seemed so important and everyone you so wanted to impress seem to just fade away and you can just bask in the love of Jesus.

Eventually, I met and married my third and current husband, and it was while living with him before we were married that I had a conversation with my local Anglican vicar. I decided to attend the local church services and became very involved in church life. I was elected onto the Parochial Church Council and eventually applied to train as a Lay Reader. I was accepted and began a three-year course, having already completed four years of other church courses.

I found it very hard to get into the institution of the church and once in it found myself constantly wondering how it all related to Jesus and His ministry. The first time I managed to get through the door of a church I felt uncomfortable and very nervous. The same thing happened when I eventually plucked up the courage to go to Bible study. Everyone I seemed to meet had been going to church since childhood, been in the choir, and had certainly not led the colourful life I had. Eventually, I left and vowed never to set foot in a Christian institution again.

But underneath it all I knew there was something missing and I continued to search for the 'something' that would give meaning and purpose to my life. I went on a trip to Iona with a Celtic spirituality group expecting to find some answers in that wonderfully 'spiritual place', but went home much as I had arrived, still searching. I also visited the Northumbria Community and again had a good week but nothing life-changing happened there. I started to attend weekly Buddhist meditations and became very interested. This culminated in my going on a retreat to a temple in Cumbria for a weekend which was aimed at recruiting people to that faith. I returned realizing that it was not quite what I was looking for, although quite what I was looking for still eluded me. The Celtic group used to have a week away each year living in community and exploring different things. I joined them for several years. They moved away from their Christian Celtic roots and have become very 'New Age'. I know all about energy-giving crystals, healing drum-bowls and Tarot cards. When they decided to go to Glastonbury to meet the High Priestess of Avalon I felt that it was time to leave.

It didn't matter where I went or what I did, something was missing from my life and I became ever more dissatisfied with my lot. Life was becoming quite grim and with family problems and a job that demanded more than I felt able to give, I was struggling to cope. My everyday phrase became 'there must be more to life than this'. Anti-depressants didn't help and the ability to consume ever-larger quantities of alcohol just left me with a headache.

After a while I found myself attending a Christian fellowship and I immediately sensed that there was something special about these people. They had something that I wanted, that I had been looking for. So, what was it? Well, they clearly loved the Lord Jesus Christ and gave their all to Him. They embraced me with all my problems. They prayed for me and with me and I have seen the prayers of an obedient and faithful people answered on my behalf. Things in my life and that of my family started to change for the better and gradually I began to realize what was missing from my life and why I had been unable to find it: all the decisions I made were for me and about me. I had been paying lip-service to a faith that I had managed to tailor to my life-style and if Jesus featured anywhere it was in my head and certainly not in my heart. While I was managing to present a solid front to everyone around me I couldn't deceive myself and I knew that the inner being was very shallow. I had been carrying an enormous rucksack of sin and wrongdoing on my back, which was dragging me down and causing me so much pain that I was hurting other people around me, even those I loved. Suddenly I realized that I didn't have to carry that load. Jesus had taken my rucksack to the cross of Calvary and died a cruel and agonising death so that I would never have to carry that burden again. He had paid the price for me because He loves me so much. What an awesome thing to do for someone like me, someone so unworthy – it takes your breath away just to think about it. There is a verse of a hymn that I find myself humming a lot without realizing it:

> Turn your eyes upon Jesus.
> Look full in his wonderful face,
> And the things of earth will grow strangely dim,
> In the light of his glory and grace.

I thank God that He led me to TCM Baptist Church where Hugh was the pastor. I found TCM to be a biblically-based church, providing sound Bible teaching, Christ-centred worship and genuine Christian fellowship. Although my family worries, a difficult job and so on are still present, I have found that I am not dealing with them alone, and I no longer live my life by myself. Jesus is sharing my life and He loves me so much that He died for me and He wants to be with me always to protect and guide me. I am so thankful that I could be baptised into Christ, and at my baptismal service I summed up my sense of gratitude by saying: 'Jesus I am sorry for the life I have led. Thank You for dying on the cross for me so that I might live. Jesus I love You and want You to be with me forever. Thank You for giving me the opportunity to be baptised and leave the old behind and start a new life in You. Thank You, Jesus.'

A Registered General Nurse
Major Garry Walker,
Postgraduate Diploma Counselling, Postgraduate Certificate Cognitive Behavioural Therapy

My eyes began to fill with tears as I sat there thinking of Debrilla, Wayne Edwards and the Italian drivers of the Aid truck. 'For God so loved the world . . . '

I was the oldest of five children, born in the mid-fifties and brought up in a Catholic family living in the west coast of Scotland. It was an unremarkable childhood, much the same as most working-class folk of that post-war era. There was a mixture of relative poverty, care-free childhood experiences and an optimism of the future.

Church for me was about getting up on a Sunday morning, putting a penny in the plate and feeling quite good about it – and maybe lighting a candle for a relative that had passed away. I made my 'First Communion' and was 'Confirmed' by the Bishop at a service with the rest of my ten-year-old classmates in Dumbarton. We sang hymns that seemed to me like religious wallpaper – they didn't inspire me or open my heart. So, for me, Jesus was forty-five minutes on a Sunday.

At the age of fifteen, blissfully ignorant of what I was letting myself in for, I joined the Medical Branch of the Army. A school friend had a brother in the Royal Artillery and as he wanted to sign up he asked me to go with him to the Sauchiehall Street recruiting office. I was gently seduced into joining at the same time; such was the power of persuasion of the recruiting sergeant!

In January, 1971, I found myself at the Royal Army Medical Apprentices' College in Ashvale, Surrey. It was here that I first met Major Ken Sears, the officer commanding the unit. An ex-Parachute Regiment medic and reformed alcoholic, he had become a Christian many years earlier and ran the College with a strong Christian ethos: an assembly three times a week commencing with a prayer, a short Bible reading and a closing hymn, with a compulsory church service in your own denomination on the Sunday. However, for me Christianity was still just forty-five minutes on a Sunday.

Posted to Catterick at seventeen years of age, I was a 'big boy' now and no longer had to go to church on a Sunday, though I enjoyed warm friendship from the Christian organisation Sandes Soldiers' Homes, which provided cups of tea and sticky buns and a weekly Bible study for lonely young men like me. But, it was really just the same as I had been doing for the forty-five minutes on a Sunday. It wasn't that I didn't believe, it just didn't seem important or relevant to me.

Some years later I was posted to Ireland during the times of 'the troubles'. Two of the soldiers with me were killed by the IRA and I thought to myself, 'I wonder where Christ is?'

Then it was the Gulf War. 'Desert Storm' was a great challenge to the British Army in terms of the preparation for deployment. The logistics of getting such a large force on the ground and ensuring that the correct levels of equipment were readily available – fuel, food, water, medical supplies, munitions, nuclear, chemical, and biological protection suits, respirators, NBC alarms, decontamination kits, and more – was an immense task for the planners but one in which they succeeded. It's easy think of it now as the '100-hour war', but to do so greatly undermines the efforts of so many troops deployed in that operation. The Field Psychiatric Team was deployed in October, 1990. We had a peripatetic role, initially based with 33 Field Hospital in Al Jubal, before moving into the desert with the divisional troops at the end of November, 1990.

The media and politicians had hyped-up the war and there was an expectation that the Iraqi army possessed significant chemical and biological munitions, and that the mortality rates among the allies would be high. I attended several church services in the desert conducted by Army padres and was struck by the increase in the number attending as the closeness of our attack date on Iraq grew closer. The night before we went into Iraq, not knowing what to expect, I prayed: 'Lord, I hope You are with me.' But I hadn't repented for my sins, I hadn't asked Jesus to take control over my life. I was His 'fair-weather friend'.

We went into Iraq and travelled over to Kuwait very quickly, which was an answer to many people's prayers, but as I witnessed the death and pain, both physical and mental, I wondered what the sense was behind that. What was God's plan for all of that?

In April, 1993, as the only army mental health worker in this particular theatre, I was deployed on my first tour of Bosnia based in Vitez. Similar to the Gulf War, I had a roving remit to visit all of the locations either informally for general stress education or to see patients and advise medical officers and unit commanders on the suitability of medevacing to the UK those experiencing psychological problems on operations, or treating them in their location in theatre. This was a very difficult tour for the outgoing Cheshire Regiment, commanded by Lt. Colonel Bob Stewart. They had witnessed many atrocities during their six months there. They were succeeded by the Prince of Wales's Own Regiment of Yorkshire, commanded by Lt. Col Alastair Duncan, who, likewise, had an extremely challenging time. Both regiments and the supporting servicemen and women can look back with great pride at their achievements in Bosnia.

One of the first sights to greet you when you travelled from Tomisladagrad to Gornji Vakuf

en-route to Vitez and Tuzla was the memorial stone
at the bridge across the river dedicated to Wayne
Edwards who was attached to the Cheshires. He was
killed by a sniper in February, 1993, while on patrol
in his armoured vehicle: one pointless death out of
thousands who were killed, murdered or injured in
that conflict. I remember Debrilla, our young
Serbian interpreter based in the camp at Vitez, one
minute translating for wounded Muslim women and
children in the small British Army surgical facility,
then just hours later killed by a sniper's bullet in the
doorway of the house in the camp where she stayed.
I saw three Italian relief lorry drivers who had been
bringing food and medical aid to those in most need
who had been dragged out of their vehicles and
murdered for their cargo on the road to Vitez.
Three days later as we picked up the three lifeless
bodies my thoughts were, 'How can you believe in
a God when He lets these things happen to good
people? Where's the sense in that? Where were You
then, God?'

Later, as I was working as an Army Community
Psychiatric Nurse at the Queen Elizabeth Military
Hospital, my family was living in Woolwich in South
East London. During many of my times away my
wife, Carolyn, attended the Slade Evangelical Church
in Plumstead. They provided a weekday meeting for
mothers and toddlers to get together without force-
feeding those attending with religion. This led to
Carolyn attending the Sunday services and becoming
a Christian. Eventually I was dragged along to taxi/
control our four young children and, disturbingly for
me, found that they were a friendly, normal bunch

of people with a great love of Christ. The minister, Hugh Hill, was a powerful orator. He gave a consistently strong message from the Bible, which was difficult to ignore. The hymns and worship songs were a mixture of the traditional and the new. I found some of the newer worship songs very moving, especially after my experience in Bosnia. For example, a verse from Graham Kendrick's 'From Heaven You Came (*The Servant King*)':

Come see His hands and His feet.
The scars that speak of sacrifice;
Hands that flung stars into space
To cruel nails surrendered.

Around this time, in 1994, I attended a reunion with some Army friends who were with me at the Army Apprentice College in the seventies. We had a great time renewing old friendships with lots of long forgotten photographs, followed by a formal dinner in the evening and a thanksgiving service on the Sunday taken by Ken Sears, my old Commanding Officer. Ken was a leading figure in the Soldiers' and Airmen's Scripture Readers Association (SASRA) in Aldershot at that time. During the service Ken related a story about a Scripture Reader visiting a family whose son had been killed in the Gulf War. The boy's mother thanked him for his consoling words of comfort but said, 'Where was your God when my son was killed?' Sitting in the comfortable, relative darkness of that service I thought to myself – *exactly!* Ken then struck the audience and me with the Scripture Reader's reply to the distraught mother with a comment that stopped my cynical thoughts instantly, 'God was exactly in the same place with your son as He was with His own Son when He died on Calvary.' The impact of this statement struck me like a spear in my heart. My eyes began to fill with tears as I sat there thinking of Debrilla, Wayne Edwards and the Italian drivers of the Aid truck. *'For God so loved the world . . . '*

A month or two later Hugh Hill visited my wife and me at our Army quarter in Woolwich. We had the usual chit-chat over a cup of tea and Hugh suddenly asked me, 'If you were to die tonight, Garry, where would you go?' I sort of shifted uncomfortably in my seat as I thought of an answer. I could not in all honesty reply 'to heaven with God'; for I knew in my heart I'd just been going through the motions, just hovering on the fringes of real Christianity. This question, 'Where was I going after death?' was a great challenge to me and not one that I had ever given any thought to. I then accepted Hugh's invitation to attend a short Bible study course with other like-minded people. The course asked and answered many of the questions I had about God, Jesus, and the way of salvation. And following this experience, in July, 1995, I accepted the Lord Jesus as my personal Saviour. Baptism followed very soon afterwards at the Slade Church.

My profession of faith was one of the most difficult things I have ever done because it meant me losing control over my life and giving it to the Lord Jesus.

The years have passed since that fateful night in Plumstead and I have been blessed with a Christian marriage and home. Today I work as the Head of

Clinical Service with the charity Combat Stress (also known as The Ex-Services Mental Welfare Society), at their treatment centre in Ayrshire, Scotland. They were established in 1919 after the Great War to deal with those affected by the aftermath of warfare. We have over 1,500 veterans who come to Hollybush House from all over Scotland, Ireland and the North of England for treatment – predominantly for post-traumatic stress disorder.

My one regret after seventeen years is that I did not ask Jesus into my life sooner.

A Mother and Shop Owner
Debbie Prevett – Wife

Things hit rock bottom when one day after being let down in a relationship I suddenly realized that I didn't have a life. I became very depressed and feeling that I could not live with the things I had done I seriously considered suicide.

It is fifteen years since I became a Christian and it took me twenty-nine years before that to realize that God loved me.

I grew up in an atheist home where my Dad told me there was no God so, as most children do when their parents tell them something, I believed it. At the age of twenty-one I bought my first house and left home to move in with my boyfriend who I subsequently married three years later. It was shortly after this that things started to go wrong. Wanting to be loved the way I was and not to be changed into

the person my husband really wanted, I began
cheating on him because I was looking for happiness.
The more I cheated, the worse I felt, until about a
year after I got married I decided I couldn't carry on
with it and left my husband to start a new life,
thinking that I wouldn't be trapped and could be
on my own.

That was when my life took a nose-dive from
bad to worse. I had never felt so unhappy and lonely.
I went in and out of relationships looking for
happiness but never found it. I tried different jobs,
including working in pubs, thinking this might help
me meet people. I moved house ten times in two
years, but nothing worked. Things hit rock-bottom
when, one day after being let down in a relationship,
I suddenly realized that I didn't have a life. I became
very depressed and feeling that I could not live with
the things I had done I seriously considered suicide.
The devil was there reminding me of all the wrong
things I had done and that when I was born I wasn't
wanted: my real mother had left me in the hospital.
He made me feel that no one loved or cared for me.
Every day I got up I could not forget the past. I
wanted to die. Then, one night when I had had
enough, I got on my knees and begged a God I did
not believe in to let me die and release me from my
miserable life.

By this time I was working at the National
Maritime Museum in Greenwich. My manager was a
Christian and despite my insults and jokes about him
being a 'man of the cloth' or a 'Bible basher' he
continued to invite me to his church until eventually
I said yes (adding that I would sit at the back and if

anyone 'got heavy' I would be off!). However, I was
very surprised at what I experienced in the church
service; everyone was so kind and helpful and they
all seemed 'normal'. The people were all so peaceful
and I realized they had something that I didn't have
and I wanted to find out more. But shortly after I
started going to church my health deteriorated and,
while I was waiting for diagnosis and treatment, I fell
away from church attendance.

It was about six months later when I returned to
work that I discovered one of my colleagues went
to a church near my home and I asked him if he
would meet me at the Slade Evangelical Church in
Plumstead.

That visit led to me attending regularly and a few
months later I realized that Jesus not only forgave
my past sins but He forgot them too, and with Jesus
in my life I found the happiness I had been looking
for. I could now live with myself because I realized
that I was not alone anymore and that Jesus loved
me despite all the things I had done.

Within a few months of my life-changing
experience I met Peter, a Catholic, who had vowed
never to go to church again. However, maybe
because of his interest in me he came along to
church on Sundays and soon he, too, was attending
a Bible study class led by Hugh, which led to him
becoming a Christian. Shortly after that we were
married by Hugh. At last I had realized that I had to
let God have control. I now know that the Lord
chose Peter because he knew the type of person I
needed and I finally gave everything over to the
Lord and surrendered my life to Him.

I have been happily married to Peter for thirteen
years and we have two wonderful children. We now
live in Bude, Cornwall, and are part of an Elim
church which is making a real impact on this
community. Life still has its ups and downs but I
know I am never alone. The scripture given to me at
my baptism sums everything up for me:

> *'I sought the* Lord, *and he answered me;*
>   *he delivered me from all my fears.'*
>
> (Psalm 34:4)

If you do not believe that Jesus is the Way, the Truth
and the Life, then I would ask you to think long and
hard before you turn away. I found Jesus the hard
way; I had to hit rock bottom before I would ask for
His help. Talk to Jesus today before life takes
another downward turn.

CHAPTER 14

WOULD YOU
DO IT THIS WAY
AGAIN?

*'If you want to walk on water, you have to get out
of the boat.' In some ways I think that's what I did
and I'm not sure you would get a very sensible
theological answer from Peter if you asked him
why he got out of the boat.*

The baptismal testimonies you have just read are four
of many I have had the privilege of sharing, and help
answer the question I am often asked: 'Would you do it all
again?'

The unspoken inference is that perhaps my Christian experience should have been quieter and not so dramatic, and then we might not have lost our printing company and home with all the trauma and upheaval it caused our family, friends, employees and others. It is a fair question. So, would I do things the same way again?

With the benefit of hindsight, theological training and ministry experience, I would now probably be more cautious and less willing to respond to my feelings, and be more careful about walking through doors that miraculously opened in answer to prayer.

But you have to appreciate the quite astonishing way that God moved into my life and the amazing answers to prayer. As a new Christian exposed to circumstances that many mature Christians have never experienced, it's not so easy to be matter-of-fact, although I do think at times I ran before I could walk, so to speak.

For me it wasn't abstract theory, it was reality. The events recorded in chapter 8 happened as I have described. Verse 9 of Acts 16 records the apostle Paul having a vision of a man of Macedonia begging him to visit that country and help them. You do not then read that Paul had a debate as to whether such a thing was possible ... No! Scripture records, '*After Paul had seen the vision, we got ready at once to leave for Macedonia* ... ' (Acts 16:10).

All I can say is that God moved and answered my prayers in the most extraordinary ways often leaving me with no thought of weighing up the options. Think of the generation of Israelites who walked through the Red Sea without getting their feet wet, yet due to their lack of faith spent forty years in the wilderness and did not enter the Promised Land. It's been said, 'If you want to walk on water, you have to get out of the boat.' In some ways I think that's what I did and I'm not sure you would get a very sensible theological answer from Peter if you asked him why he got out of the boat.

I take comfort in the belief that if a Christian makes a decision that they believe to be God-honouring, yet somehow they've got it wrong (after all we're not perfect, we do make mistakes of judgment), then surely God's promise from Romans 8:28 comes in to play: *'In all things God works for the good of those who love him.'* To me that means if you believe that it is right and according to biblical principles then 'get on with it!' And if that means moving out of our comfort zones, 'letting go and letting God', then with the assurance that God knows the motives of our hearts we can't lose, for He will work it for good.

I lost nothing of lasting value: God's love is not measured by the success or failure of a printing company. What then have I gained? An intimacy and knowledge of God that is beyond price and the privilege of working for Him in proclaiming His gospel message which will reward me throughout eternity.

In 2 Corinthians 11:30 Paul says:

'If I must boast, I will boast of the things that show my weakness.'

I've told you some of my weaknesses and there are many more. But listen. I have pastored three evangelical churches – in Sussex, inner-city London and city-centre Lincoln – where I, by God's grace, have led many men and women to Jesus, delighted in their baptism and encouraged them to find and use their spiritual gifts for the building up of the Church. I have inducted elders and deacons, sent out men and women to the mission field, been involved in setting up ministries throughout every age-group in the Church, enjoyed leading vibrant, growing Christian fellowships and had a leading role in city-wide evangelistic events that have touched the lives of thousands. I have preached the gospel and given my testimony to the love of God in Germany, Italy, Romania, Africa, India, Afghanistan and America – and I have no doubt whatsoever that it is all due to the grace, love and mercy of my Lord Jesus Christ.

The bottom line is this: if I had been left in my former life-style, I would by now be dead, in hospital, in prison or living as an embittered lonely alcoholic in some dingy flat. Whereas, by accepting Christ's gift of salvation and His invitation to follow Him, I have enjoyed a loving marriage, a terrific family life with three great children and an exciting and fulfilling work, which has brought me genuine friends the length and breadth of the country. And, even more, I can look forward with complete assurance to walking through the Valley of the Shadow of Death holding the nail-pierced hand of the Good Shepherd and enjoying His company in glory throughout eternity – you can't beat that!

What about you? Are you willing to get out of the boat and follow Him?

About the Author

Having retired from the full-time pastoral ministry Hugh is currently employed by FIEC (the Fellowship of Independent Churches), and with his wife, Joyce, administers the Bible School PfS North. Hugh also travels throughout the UK helping churches to focus on the spiritual priorities of gospel ministry and mission. He is happy to reply to any questions raised by this book and is available to speak at appropriate meetings.

He can be contacted at:

H & J Publishing Ltd
8 Albion Crescent
Lincoln LN1 1EB
Email: hugh@hughhill.co.uk

Further copies of this book can be obtained via the website:

www.hjpublishing.co.uk